CONTENTS

Acknowledgements

I would like to thank the Reverend Duncan Finlayson and the late Mrs. Jean Finlayson for their patience and advice. Without their support this book would not exist. Many thanks to Sarah Grant and Lynne Sperandeo of the National Children's Homes Association for their help and support. Thanks to Eric Fowell for his encyclopaedic knowledge of Rushden and the photographs of Northampton Town F.C. and Queen Street; to the staff at the "Evening Telegraph" office in Rushden; to Ian Clarkson for writing the foreword; to Phil Vasili for his advice and encouragement. Finally thanks to Tony for his bookseller's knowledge.

Preface

On Thursday 21st March 1918, the German Army launched "Operation Michael" or the Kaiserschlacht, the Kaiser's Battle. On the Somme, following a massive bombardment, the Germans drove back the Allied 3rd and 5th Armies and retook the ground lost at such cost in 1916.

Thus began the Allies "March Retreat" and for their commanders the problems of successful withdrawal and a morale boosting rearguard action. Thousands of lives were lost on both sides in vicious hand-to-hand trench fighting, counter attacks against the German line and ubiquitous shelling. On the whole front it is estimated that the British lost over 160,000 men in just sixteen days, the French 77,000 and the Germans at least equal to the Allies' combined total.

One of the British victims was a recently transferred second lieutenant, nothing unusual in that, junior officers were expendable and their life expectancy during a battle measured in hours even minutes. This particular junior officer was popular with his men, intelligent, brave, again nothing unusual. He had been ordered to lead his men in an attack on the German trenches at Favreuil and soon after the attack began, only metres into No Man's Land, the officer fell wounded. His men, under heavy fire from the German machine guns, made attempts to get him back to cover. Unfortunately these efforts were in vain and the officer died from his wounds.

Nothing unusual, one man's life set against the casual and devastating carnage of the First World War. Nothing except that this officer was black. The first black man commissioned as a combat officer. His name was Walter Tull.

Introduction

Several books have been published in recent years about the roles of black footballers. Notable amongst these is Phil Vasili's biography of Arthur Wharton, Preston North End's sometime goalkeeper and amateur athletic champion. By the same author, "Colouring over the White Line", a compendium of black footballers who over the years established themselves as professionals, men such as Wharton, Alfred Charles and Roy Brown. Other titles include Dave Bowler's and Jas Bains',"Samba at the Smethwick End" which concentrates on West Brom's famous "Three Degrees": Laurie Cunningham, Cyrille Regis and Brendan Batson. Supporters over the age of thirty will remember their contribution to the successful Baggies' side of the late 70's and early 80's.
All the players mentioned have been victims of racism and have done something to break down the walls of prejudice either because of their dignity in the face of provocation or through the sheer talent that forced their detractors to swallow their words. One such man was W.D.J. Tull who through willpower and discipline pushed the barriers in professional sport and in another bastion of racism the British Army.
Walter Tull's story for many people came to light during July 1999, when several dozen people gathered at the south end of Northampton Town's Sixfields Stadium. They were there to celebrate the opening of a garden of remembrance in Tull's honour and to pay tribute to a remarkable man. A remarkable man whose brief life ended on the 25th March 1918. A result of the German offensive called "Operation Michael" or Kaiserlachlact. A desperate effort by the Germans to turn the tide of the war before the full effect of American involvement could be felt. Thousands of lives were lost, a combined total of some half a million men from both sides.
No-one could know what those lost lives may have realised, Walter's influence at least has reverberated down the years.

Foreword

It is a real honour to be asked to write a foreword for such an amazing man.
Nowadays all of us are entitled to freedom within our lives and this is due in no small way to people like Walter Tull. Walter fought for his country to ensure that people like me were free to ply my trade for Northampton some eighty years after his death at the tender age of twenty nine.
Tull was also a groundbreaker in race relations and in an era when black people weren't as readily accepted as now became the first black footballer to don a Cobblers' shirt. Not only that but he was talented enough to catch the eye of the legendary Herbert Chapman, who was the Alex Ferguson of his era.
I have been fortunate enough to experience an increasingly more tolerant attitude during my time as a footballer because people are now judged on their ability as footballers, not the colour of their skin. However, I was a supporter on the terraces in the 1970's and recall the often diabolical abuse that was served up on an almost weekly basis to black players.
Walter Daniel Tull crammed an awful lot into his short life and Cobblers' fans should be privileged to know that they had a real man of bravery within their ranks. We often speak about footballers showing bravery on the field of play but Tull not only fought for his country but also showed real bravery on the pitch every time he stepped on to play.
I will never forget the sacrifices that Tull made to enable me to play at Wembley with Northampton on two occasions with black players appearing for both teams and wearing their shirts with pride, their colour not even being an issue.
As a player I am aware of the memorial that was built in Walter's memory and all present day players should be thankful for the unprecedented show of strength by people like Walter Tull.
His memory should stay with us for ever.
Ian Clarkson ex-Northampton Town FC August 2002

Chapter One

Walter's story begins on the island of Barbados the birthplace of his father Daniel, from whom Walter received his second name and birthplace of his paternal grandparents Anna and William. Both Anna (nee Lashley) and William had been born into slavery - this shows the huge divide Walter had bridged from slavery to commissioned officer in his majesty's army in two generations!

When Daniel was born the family lived on the Clifton estate in the parish of St. Thomas. They moved a few years later to St. Michael's Parish. Although no official records survive, Daniel was probably born during the early 1850's and had a brother and a sister. He grew up in a close knit and loving family environment and initially was taught to read by his mother. As Phil Vasili notes in "Colouring Over the White Line", a law was passed in 1676 which forbade the teaching of Christianity to blacks in case it gave them ideas above their station or ideas about equality or improvement. As far as Anna was concerned improvement was the key, she sent her son to a Methodist missionary school where he received a basic education. It appears that at some point Daniel had some extra tuition from his cousin Henry Simmons, who claimed the title Bachelor of Arts. Thus armed he looked to find a trade.

Daniel was initially apprenticed to a man named Giddins but after eight months he switched to work for Joseph Massiah, husband of one of his cousins. In a brief diary that Daniel kept he refers to Massiah as, "A good workman; but a cruel man to his apprentices." He went on to describe the floggings meted out for trivial oversights there, "...was scarcely a week pass over my head but for what I did not have a thrashing from him." Nevertheless Daniel improved and stayed with Massiah for over three years. At this point Daniel asked for an increase on his sixpence a week wages. Massiah refused and so Daniel left to join another carpenter.

Unfortunately Massiah refused to pay Daniel his last wages and so Daniel decided to confront his tormentor. "I went to his house with a determination to get my money or else give him a thrashing man as he was." The confrontation did not occur, Massiah wisely kept a low profile. Frustrated, Daniel returned home and in his own words, "made severe abuses," much to the disgust of his father who harangued the young man for leaving his apprenticeship and for his ungodly language. Daniel received another thrashing for his pains and resolved to leave home, "So from this time I vowed in my mind I would leave home or I told my mother I would because of my father mistaken I little thought then that it would come true afterward as it did so in the course of time."(sic)

Having completed his apprenticeship with a colleague of Massiah's, Daniel soon discovered higher wages were on offer on the neighbouring island of St. Lucia. Anna used the family's meagre savings to help kit Daniel out with clothes and tools and the young man set sail on the 11th August 1873. Quickly establishing himself a skilled and willing worker Daniel saved the majority of his money to send home. Although the wages were reasonable at some point Daniel saw a better opportunity for advancement, emigration to Britain. Perhaps there was something of a wanderer in Daniel or perhaps the missionaries had instilled a sense of the importance of and opportunities available in the mother country, because in 1876 Daniel decided to sail to England. After much searching he was able to find a berth as a ship's carpenter and thus paid for his own passage.

Emigration was and is a massive undertaking requiring money and contacts - in the mid nineteenth century it was not unusual for the poor to seek a better life. Opportunities were sought in the USA, Australia but Great Britain was still a magnet for many inhabitants of British colonies. Irish emigrants looked to America, but Daniel looked towards England. He had a trade and possibly from his early education and dealings with the missionary workers contacts.

A modern reader might think that Daniel would be making his way to an England with little or no black community but this was not the case. The first blacks came to London in the mid sixteenth century as a result of trade with Africa. They came as slaves to the wealthy, by the end of the century Elizabeth I was advising the civic authorities that there were blackamores, "of which kinde there are already here too manie." The trade also meant that black crews of the many merchant ships from Africa found temporary or permanent homes in London.

Many black people had arrived as a result of the infamous slave triangle. Ships left the ports of Liverpool and Bristol laden with textiles and other goods. On the African coast these goods were traded for slaves and thence on to the West Indies to swap their human cargoes for sugar, cotton, tobacco and rum. Inevitably slaves came back to Britain to work in the grand houses of the aristocracy, some arrived as stowaways, some had been given freedom for fighting for Empire during the American War of Independence. Fears and anxieties about the number of black people were not confined to the Tudor monarchy. John Fielding writer and J.P. suggested that they were a subversive influence in the city. During the mid to late eighteenth century immigrants were settling in such areas as Wapping and St Giles.

By 1787 the black population of London alone was believed to have been 20,000. Not all of them were slaves or servants, many joined the army, became entertainers, the Duchess of Queensberry, for example, employed a man called Soubise as a fencing teacher. Unfortunately many of the immigrants especially the black recruits who fought for the English in the American War of Independence soon found themselves destitute. The problem was considered serious enough to set up a committee of repatriation. Echoes of the 1960's and Enoch Powell? Many historians have suggested that by the beginning of the nineteenth century the black population was a familiar presence on the streets. They had become, for the most part, a part of the underclass. Thus finding a "home" for those loyalists and freed slaves became an urgent priority and ran in tandem with the efforts of the authorities who wanted to clear the overcrowded jails of that period. Sights were thus turned to Australia and Sydney Cove and to Sierra Leone. It seems that the twentieth first century does not have the copyright when it comes to equating black and crime.

One particular barrier existed in the ability of blacks to better their lot - the barring of blacks from taking apprenticeships - this was at least one area Daniel did not have to worry about.

Daniel, directed by his Methodist connections, settled in Folkestone and with their help found lodgings and work. A surviving letter from his mother shows him sending money home.

"My Dear Son,

I return our most humble thanks for your gift…it was very acceptable. I do assure you, for I want something to pay Henry's compliment and our little hut wanted great repairs so it came in good to aid these purposes; we are very thankful too of receiving your portrait. It has bring(sic) great delight to family and friends that have seen it, ours you must excuse us of sending this time seeing the statement of our condition, how your assistance is appropriate." Later she thanked him for a pound, a considerable sum at the time when the average weekly wage for a working man was not much more. Anna's faith shines through as she commended her son, "into the hands of our heavenly father who seeth, and knows all things, may his spirit thrive with you and strengthen your work of salvation in Christ."

A sad footnote to this letter dated 29th December, 1878 was that Mrs. Simmons, Daniel's Godmother, was ill and might not survive until his next letter.

Whilst living in Folkestone, Daniel began to attend the Grace Hill Wesleyan Chapel and it is probable that whilst attending the Sunday services Alice Palmer first caught his eye; their relationship able to develop with the frequent social events, teas and classes organized by the chapel.

Unusually for the period the Palmer parents did not appear to object to the growing relationship between their daughter and a black man. Given the stiff Victorian values and beliefs about inferiority of the black character this displays a refreshing sense of equality and fair mindedness. A cynic might suggest given their humble backgrounds they saw financial opportunity. The Palmers were agricultural labourers, money almost certainly in short supply, possibly relying on tied accommodation. Schooling would have played little part in the Palmers' lives, which would revolve around backbreaking work in the week and worship on Sunday. Daniel represented something of a catch for Alice, good looking (if we give him some credit for Walter's appearance), educated, religious and with a trade. Daniel was welcomed into the Palmer household!

Alice's mother wrote to Daniel in reply to his proposal to marry her daughter, she began warmly.

"Dearest Child,

I daresay you think me cruel and unkind in not answering your kind and welcome letter and was most happy to hear you were better and fit for work…you have asked for my only daughter you are welcome if it is to contribute to her happiness and yours as well I feel as much interested in one's happiness as I do in the others…but there are two things I must beg of you and the first is of the most importance that you will be kind to her for she is a tender plant and is wanted a deal of care in raising and the other is you will never take her out of England, whilst I am alive do not think, Dan in wishing these two things that I doubt your love for her and that your actions have shown your respect for the family but I suppose it is a mother's tender feelings over the only tender female plant my heavenly father has been pleased to spare me." Like his own mother she aired her faith, asking that both would ask for assistance from heaven to help in their future together.

By 1891 the now married Alice and Daniel had settled into Walter Road, Folkestone and were soon parents of a growing family of three boys and two daughters, sadly their first child, Bertha Susanna born in 1891, died in infancy. The boys, William the eldest son, named after his grandfather was followed by Edward and Walter. The girls Cecilia (Cissie) and Elsie [1] completed the family. Money may have been scarce but the family was a happy one. Life revolved around the church and as Edward would later remark, the children had their Sunday School and the parents their Church and for them Sunday was the day of the week. Unfortunately for the children their lives were soon to be devastated as their mother died, on the 14th April 1895, of cancer. She was 42, even for those times a tragically young age to die and especially leaving a young family. William was not yet twelve, Cecilia ten, Edward eight, Walter six, and Elsie only three years of age.

Daniel quickly found a surrogate mother for the children close at hand in Clara, Alice's cousin - they married but within a short space of time Daniel also died of heart disease. Just before his death he fathered a sixth child, Clara gave birth to a daughter, Miriam Victoria, in October 1897, just two short months before his death on the 10th December. Clara was left in a desperate situation with six children to care for and little money available. Daniel had earned a modest enough wage and Alice's illness had made huge demands on the few savings they had. In the two years together Daniel and Clara had struggled to make ends meet. William the eldest boy was working as a carpenter's apprentice and was bringing seven shillings into the house. The weekly rent amounted to six shillings if the two girls looked after Miriam, Clara might find

1 *In later life Elsie was awarded the British Empire Medal for services to the local Folkestone Hospital.*

Clockwise from right, Cissie on Daniel's knee, Walter, Elsie, William and Edward

a job even so the outlook was extremely grim. Daniel's will made it clear just how little he had: date 11th November 1897, he left his tools to William, with the stipulation that if either Walter or Edward became carpenters then the tools would be equally divided. The effects of Alice amounting to two rings, a silver thimble and some baby clothes would be shared by Elsie, Cissie and Miriam. A poignant addition was that William should do all he could to keep a home together for all the family and, "…in any case Bill is not to neglect the girls."

Clara had no-one to turn to, the Palmer grandparents were dead, the nearest surviving family, aunts and uncles were hardly much better off than she was. William Palmer, who lived near Dover, was a farm labourer earning fourteen shillings a week. Robert Palmer, who was also a labourer, earned the same. Finally, John Palmer from Dover, worked on the land as a casual worker, all had families and only sympathy to spare.

In desperation Clara turned to the church for help and advice and it was the minister of Grace Hill chapel, where Daniel met Alice, who came to the rescue. The Reverend George Adcock ensured that the chapel's funds covered the rent. He then contacted the Parish Guardians and secured an initial payment of five shillings and ten pence for the children's upkeep. With William's wage, the family had a collective income of twelve and ten pence, not enough for seven mouths to feed. Daniel had, at least, taken a form of insurance with the Prudential Assurance Company, but the £16 it paid out on his death was completely exhausted by medical and funeral expenses.

The Reverend Adcock came to the rescue again, if the family were to survive he suggested that Walter and Edward should be sent to the Children's Home and Orphanage in Bethnal Green. This was a Methodist organization, founded in 1869 by the Reverend Thomas Bowman Stephenson, Francis Horner and Alfred Mager. They wanted to provide education, training and perhaps most importantly a good home for the orphans and destitute children whom they had come across on the streets of London. The Home's motto was, "To Seek And To Save That Which Is Lost". Clara became ill herself and weighed down by the loss of Daniel reluctantly agreed that the boys' welfare would be best served if they left Folkestone. She was no stereotypical, evil stepmother unloading her spouse's children onto an uncaring world. It was simply a case of genuine, urgent need, there is absolutely no doubt that Clara cared very deeply for the boys, there was simply no other choice.

Adcock undertook the arrangements and "sponsored" the boys, even then there was no guarantee they would be accepted, there was after all a great call upon the few spaces available for such care. The Bonner Road Home was always full, when vacancies arose, proof was required of the applicants' suitability. Suitability covered many things, colour was not one of them as a note to Adcock from the Home made clear: "I am obliged to you for indicating the children are coloured. The fact will not preclude a favourable decision in their case, other things being equal." [2] The boys with Adcock's backing were soon accepted but as they prepared for their new lives, Adcock received a telegram saying there was, after all, no place for Walter and Edward at the Home. The Reverend fired back an angry letter demanding that the original agreement be kept. On February 12th, 1898 he received an apology and reassurance that places existed, "Mr. Pendlebury telegraphed without reference to me, and because time pressed so that your letter could not remain until my return. In all the circumstances, of the case, however, I feel it much better that the children should come at once. There are no vacancies, but we can temporarily make arrangements by sending two other children to another Branch where the numbers are not as strictly limited as here. We will, therefore, receive the children on Monday as you are aware." [3]

2 *National Children's Home Archive*

3 *National Children's Home Archive*

Clara's illness delayed the boys' move to the home and it was left to Adcock to take them up to London on the 24th February, they made their way to Cannon Street Station, where the brothers were to be handed over to a member of staff from the Home. Adcock confirmed arrangements in writing to Mr.Pendlebury at the Home.

By agreeing to the move Clara effectively gave up all rights where the boys were concerned, she had to sign a Form of Agreement for each of them which stated:

"I pledge myself not to interfere with him in any way so long as he remains therein; and I hereby further agree to the Child being sent to any situation in this country or abroad, chosen by the said Principal. Also I promise to give every assistance in my power to the Principal and Officers in their efforts on the Child's behalf.

Further, I hereby agree not to remove the Child, without the consent of the Committee, but should I do so I hereby agree to make payment to the Treasurer for the time being, of the said Children's Home, of the outlay which shall have been expended by the Institution on the Child's behalf, at the rate of Eight Shillings per week from the time of admission." [4]

Many children who entered the Home were sent abroad as the Home at this time had initiated an emigration scheme they had begun by sending children to Canada in 1872. Later similar schemes were begun involving Australia and New Zealand. Although this sounds somewhat cruel and final, thousands of youngsters settled to a much brighter future abroad. There was no chance that this could have happened to the boys, Clara would never have agreed to such a course of action. Nevertheless, even if things improved and Clara wanted the boys back home there was the question of compensation for the home which would have certainly proved beyond Clara's grasp, as the Home's application form indicated she hoped to gain some work taking in washing. This would not feed and clothe the family and recompense the Home. It appeared the boys would be in for a long stay in care.

4 NCH Archive

It is worth noting that Bethnal Green was a tough area in the 1890's, there were many successful and highly organized gangs in operation. Historians have noted the multitude of street vendors, travellers, tramps, dog fanciers, dog stealers, sharpers and pickpockets. The police were frequently called upon to deal with robberies, domestic violence, muggings and drunkenness. Strangers were not welcomed in a close knit community. Much of the area consisted of narrow streets, dark alleyways and large, decrepit, tenement buildings which the newly formed London County Council was beginning to demolish, although it was not until the Second World War when significant changes came to the area courtesy of the Luftwaffe. One can only guess what the impact of the area had on two young boys from the relative backwater of Folkestone. Stories about nearby Whitechapel must have stirred their imaginations, it was only ten years since Jack the Ripper's grisly reign of terror during the Autumn of 1888.

Chapter Two

Before joining the Home both boys underwent medical examinations, amongst the various tests Walter was successfully vaccinated, although against what is not recorded. He was found free of Scrofula, Fits, and Cutaneous Disorder. He had had Measles but not Scarlatina or Small Pox. He had perfect use of limbs, eyesight and hearing. He was not incontinent, in fact his general health was described as very good. His character and disposition was recorded as "Honest - Truthful - Somewhat quick-tempered - afterwards repentant and generally dutiful."[5] Thus supported by the Eltham Union to the tune of four shillings a week (another thank you to the Reverend Adcock) the boys began their lives at the Bonner Road Home.

Initially the boys were taken into the reception house until an appropriate course of action was decided. After a few days they were placed in Highfield House under the care of Sister Ethel. There were several houses within the Home which was organised along the lines of many public schools of the day, providing accommodation, pastoral care and the basis for inter house competition. The houses took their names from benefactors of the institution, one such was Lord Wakefield, who was the first treasurer of the Home.

The Home was well equipped with its own print shop and bakery. It had a gymnasium and a choir room and of course a large chapel. There was also a swimming pool. Opportunities for advancement were available but first the boys had to get used to the routine of Highfield House. Sister Ethel had fifteen boys in her charge who shared three bedrooms. There was also a dining room, play room and washroom with lavatories. The sister, a courtesy rather then religious title, had accommodation comprising bed and sitting rooms. Sister Ethel was in charge of all the domestic arrangements and ensured all the children had jobs within the house. All except

5 NCH Archive

the two eldest boys or girls, (Stephenson's was a mixed home taking boys and girls) who were working children.

The day began at 6.20 a.m. when beds were made followed by a wash with cold water. On their first morning in Highfield House Walter and Edward reported to the playroom to be assigned their jobs. As newcomers they were starting at the bottom and as such were given the job of cleaning all the household's boots and shoes. When fifteen pairs and the sister's were declared acceptable, the boys were allowed breakfast.

Breakfast usually consisted of bread and margarine washed down with a mug of cocoa. Once breakfast was cleared away, the boys and Sister would walk to the chapel with the other houses for Morning Prayers. The service was conducted by the Governor and hymns were led by the choir which consisted of some forty boys and girls- both Edward and Walter would later join the choir.

Following the service the children would then attend school which was situated next door to the chapel. Lessons lasted until twelve when according to Edward a one course meal was served, “Plain wholesome feeding one would call it but the boy with taste called it many things.” (Tull-Warnock Archive) School continued in the afternoon until tea was taken at 5 p.m., before tea however each child had to have a thorough wash and be inspected by the Sister. The reward, another round of bread and margarine washed down with cocoa! For two hours after tea the children could do as they liked in the playroom until 8p.m. when they lined up for a final inspection before bed.

The shock of such a change in their lifestyle must have been awful. How they must have wanted to see Clara and their brother and sisters again. Perhaps surprisingly Edward, the older brother, was more affected. He later reported being frightened, homesick, heartbroken at being away from Folkestone. Walter was less distraught, Edward admitting that his brother was sturdier and more open to sample new ways and new places. They must have been aware how hard it was for Clara and that she would see them as often as was practicable.

In spite of the lack of money Clara made every effort to come to London to see her stepsons. One touching letter dated December 8th, 1898 addressed to the Home read:

"Dear Sir,

I should like to come and see the to (sic) little boys tomorrow Thursday as I am in Tottenham my to dear little sons the little dark boys. I hope it will not put you out and in any way as I have not been able to write before so shall arrive about 3 o'clock tomorrow afternoon.

Yours truly

Mrs Tull." [6]

The Home was usually able to grant such applications and these were quickly joined by letters from William one such addressed from Erith in Kent read:

"Dear Sir,

I write asking you if I can see my two brothers Eddie and Walter Tull on Sunday next and about what time would it be best in the afternoon as I shall be in London that day.

W. Tull" [7]

By 1900 Cissie was also requesting permission to see her brothers, by this time she was in service, working for a Mrs Broadbank in Folkestone, she had to fit her visits in to suit the convenience of her mistress.

The home was not ideal but unlike some similar institutions the carers had the children's best interests at heart. Regular visits and holidays were enjoyed by Walter and Edward and no doubt by their peers.

Whilst in the home the boys were given a basic elementary education; which would probably have been more than the majority of boys their age and class. They were also placed in work or given a trade which again would be more than most and echoes Harper Lee's *"To Kill A Mockingbird"* for when

6 NCH Archive
7 NCH Archive

Boo Radley's peers were sent to the reformed school they received a better secondary education than anyone in the state. Echoes especially of what was about to happen to Edward.

Initially although the boys missed their family they were reasonably settled, contact was maintained with Folkestone and the prospect of being shipped abroad was extremely remote. Unfortunately for Walter another major disruption to his life was about to take place.

Having been in the home for just over two years, Walter was now twelve and Edward fourteen, the boys faced the prospect of being parted. It was proposed that Edward should be adopted by a middle class family from Glasgow. The family in question the Warnocks, Mr. Warnock was a dentist whose practice was according to one source among the "poorer people". This move must have been prompted by a visit made to Glasgow by some children from the Home under the auspices of a certain Rev. J. W. Butcher the pastor of the Warnock's local church. The visit was probably to do with the Home's choir which made annual trips to other towns and cities performing in charity concerts. Edward was a prominent member of the choir and in later years was described as having a very fine baritone voice. Walter was also a choir member and had himself a good voice but he lacked his brother's discipline and control. Whatever the situation Edward must have made a profound impact upon the Warnocks as enquiries were made about the possible adoption of Edward and promises, according to Rev. Butcher, made that he would be treated as a son and trained in Mr. Warnock's profession. When the time came to leave the Home Edward was presented with a green leather covered bible, it contained the inscription: "This bible was presented to Edward A. Tull on his leaving the Children's Home Nov.8 1900."

One can only imagine the impact upon both boys, they had lost their parents, adoptive stepmother and brother and sisters and now they were to be split up with Edward taken hundreds of miles away. Walter's anguish must have been mixed with pleasure for his brother whose prospects made a massive and surprising leap forward. The news must have had a similar effect on Clara, pleasure for Edward's prospects but fears for Walter alone and perhaps fears for herself. Glasgow in those days was quite remote from Folkestone.

With the formalities completed, the Warnocks fulfilling the various demands made by the Home, these included the holding of a daily family prayer, Edward set forth to his new home. The Warnocks did not quite stick to the absolute letter of their promises to train Edward, they kept him in school first: "… we do not intend putting the boy to work at present. We consider him smart and intelligent and would like him to go to school, in order to fit him better for the occupation we desire him to follow. We trust he will be willing to do so. As regards a home we will do all in our power to make him feel in such in every sense…" [8]

The Warnocks kept their promises, Edward was enrolled at Glasgow's prestigious Allan Glen's School and part of making him feel at home was to encourage his relationship with Walter, on many occasions Warnock supplied the train fare to enable Walter to travel up to Scotland to see his brother. This must have proved reassuring to Clara and one can only imagine the pleasure it must have given the brothers to be re-united. On one occasion Mr. Warnock had to write in a very placatory tone when Walter had upset the hierarchy at the Home, perhaps his quick temper noted by the Rev. Adcock had flared up? There is, however, no record that his behaviour led to the withdrawal of permission to visit his brother.

When Mr. Warnock wasn't writing Edward was, for example on the 27th May, 1903 he wrote to the home about the prospect of Walter spending a fortnight in Glasgow:

8 NCH Archive

"Dear Sir,

I again take the liberty of writing to you concerning my brother's holidays. We should be very pleased if you would permit Walter to visit us for a fortnight. We will send his return fare on receiving a letter from you, I may also add that although I cannot be with you on Founder's Day yet I think of you and hope you will have a happy time. I keep in touch with the Home affairs by collecting and being a member of the Y.S.U. I hope you will see it convenient to allow Walter to visit us and oblige with an early reply.

I am an old boy

Edward Tull or Warnock.

P.S last time he came straight from conference thereby making it far lighter, if there is any chance of the same this year we should be deeply indebted." [9]

Edward's letter bespeaks an interest and perhaps a fondness for the establishment beyond interest in Walter's holiday. The Home seems to have done its best for both boys and without doubt they could have ended up in a far less sympathetic environment.

At the home Walter was proving to be a popular boy amongst staff and children. He began to show some prowess in the regular soccer matches and was soon representing the Home in matches against other homes and schools.

News began to improve on the domestic front as Clara remarried, she wrote to the home about the event saying that she had married a local man from Folkestone, his name William Beer. Although buoyed by the happy news, it did not signify a sufficient change in the family fortunes to allow for the removal of Walter from Bonner Road. Under the original agreement Clara would, with Walter having been in the Home for nearly five years, have had to find in the region of £100 in recompense. But things were looking up: Edward was adopted, Clara remarried, William working and, at least, Walter doing well in the Home, his popularity resulting in

9 NCH Archive

invitations from a fellow pupil to stay with him and his adoptive parents in Huddersfield. Fred Lockly Wigglesworth had been a contemporary of Walter's, Fred or Freddy was in Newcastle House at the Home and described himself as "an old chumb" (sic) of Walter. Walter apparently had stayed with the Wigglesworths before when the Home's choir had visited Huddersfield. This was by no means a hollow invitation as Fred wrote, "We will send the railway fare if Walter can come forthwith" [10]. This letter like many others speaks of the kindness of the staff and the fond regard that old boys/girls spoke of the institution, Fred enquired of Sister Adeline and apologised for his inability to attend Founder's Day, he spoke of his "Ma and Pa" sending their kind regards. As noted earlier there were far worse places to be.

Popular as he was the Guardians in Folkestone were aware of their contribution towards Walter's upkeep and by 1903 when Walter turned fifteen they were enquiring about the possibility of placing Walter in some suitable situation. The reply from the home was not entirely optimistic, admitting they would be glad to find a position it was acknowledged that Walter was "… a somewhat slow boy, or, more correctly speaking, he is not very diligent in work". It was noted that he was working in the office at the Home and beginning to equip himself for the future but if forced immediately to find a job elsewhere, "… he would not be able to keep any situation". The letter ended with perhaps an over optimistic hope that, "… we can get him as well placed as his brother" .[11]

The football at least was going well, Walter proving to be a skilful and determined centre-forward, he was beginning also to show the versatility of later years, turning out in defence as needed. He was beginning to catch the eye of local clubs and not just because of his colour.

As the months rolled on the Home was forced to consider an appropriate future for Walter. The Guardians immediately

10 NCH Archive
11 NCH Archive

after his sixteenth birthday wrote again enquiring about Walter's future, they stipulated the unusual nature of support after the sixteenth birthday asking whether there was any, "… proposal for him as to placing him in service or employment" [12]. The answer was not long forthcoming as on the twelfth of July, 1905, the Home replied saying that they had apprenticed Walter to their own Printing Department and that there was every reason to believe that he would turn out well. The Home was reluctant however to give up the maintenance payments claiming them for at least one more year saying that the Guardians had been relieved of Edward's costs due to his adoption.

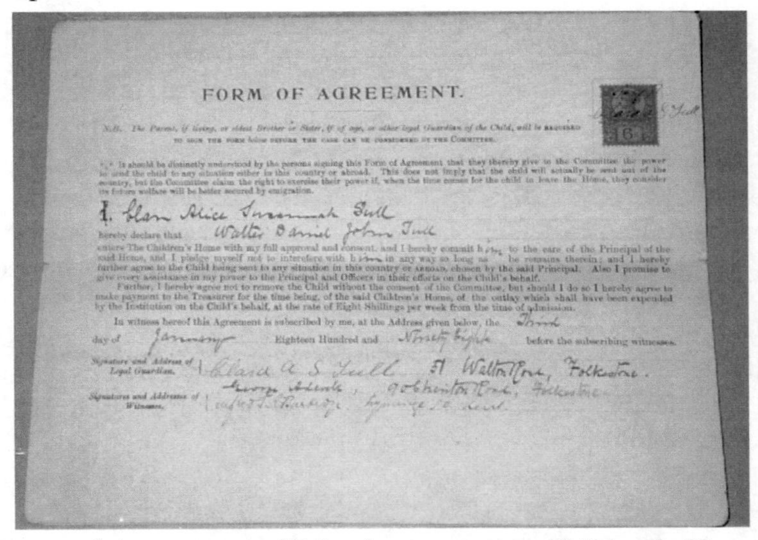

FORM OF AGREEMENT.

N.B. The Parent, if living, or eldest Brother or Sister, if of age, or other legal Guardian of the Child, will be REQUIRED TO SIGN THE FORM *below* BEFORE THE CASE CAN BE CONSIDERED BY THE COMMITTEE.

It should be distinctly understood by the persons signing this Form of Agreement that they thereby give to the Committee the power to send the child to any situation either in this country or abroad. This does not imply that the child will actually be sent out of the country, but the Committee claim the right to exercise their power if, when the time comes for the child to leave the Home, they consider its future welfare will be better secured by emigration.

I, [illegible] Alice Susannah Tull

hereby declare that Walter Daniel John Tull

enters The Children's Home with my full approval and consent, and I hereby commit him to the care of the Principal of the said Home, and I pledge myself not to interfere with him in any way so long as he remains therein; and I hereby further agree to the Child being sent to any situation in this country or ABROAD, chosen by the said Principal. Also I promise to give every assistance in my power to the Principal and Officers in their efforts on the Child's behalf.

Further, I hereby agree not to remove the Child without the consent of the Committee, but should I do so I hereby agree to make payment to the Treasurer for the time being, of the said Children's Home, of the outlay which shall have been expended by the Institution on the Child's behalf, at the rate of Eight Shillings per week from the time of admission.

In witness hereof this Agreement is subscribed by me, at the Address given below, the Third day of January Eighteen Hundred and Ninety Eight before the subscribing witnesses.

Signature and Address of Legal Guardian. [illegible] A S Tull [illegible] Walton Road, Folkestone.

Signatures and Addresses of Witnesses. [illegible]

Form of Agreement - Walter's entrance to Children's Home

Printing may have come about due to the influence of Fred Wigglesworth's family, whom Walter had stayed with in Huddersfield. The Wigglesworth's business was printing, it seems reasonable that this may have sown the idea in Walter's mind. Whatever-else it promised a safe, secure and respectable future for the boy.

12 NCH Archive

Now employed Walter was sent out into lodgings and returned to the Home's Printing Department each day. He lodged with a Mr. F. Maynard who took in other "Old Boys" from the Home. One brief note from this period is addressed to Mr. Carnegie saying, "You asked me to remind you in regard to my outfit this morning.

Yours respectfully,

W. Tull"

Presumably money was still controlled by the Home, this may be a reference to protective clothing or a general clothing allowance. There appears to have been some difficulty over food allowances paid to Maynard by the Home, leading to something of a spat between lodger and landlord. Walter claimed the cash, although Maynard insisted that Walter should take food from the lodgings. This resulted in a number of letters to the Home; the Home eventually sided with Walter and they asked Maynard in a suitable and placatory tone to allow Walter the same privileges as the older boys. Here is a typical example of Walter's clearly defined sense of what was fair and what was not and his determination not to be cowed by perceived injustice. Maybe also a hint of what Adcock had noted in his support for the boy's application to the Home - a little bit of quick temper? Nevertheless after so many years in the Home Walter could now look forward to a secure future. He had a job, some degree of independence, a loving family and many friends.

Chapter Three

Before looking at Walter's career post Bonner Road, it is important to examine that Edwardian world and to appreciate the potential barriers for a working-class 'orphan' of mixed race parentage.

We are aware of the moves made by Britain during the late eighteenth century to establish an empire. These moves continued throughout the next century in an aggressive policy of imperial conquest. Frozen out of Europe between 1792-1815 by Napoleon's machinations, Britain looked to make up for the loss of the American Colonies by pushing on in India, Africa, the Near and Far East and the Pacific Islands.

Wherever Britain colonised, the imprint of home was imposed in terms of the social hierarchies. David Carradine in his book "Ornamentalism" indicates that in the British Empire, class and status were at least as important as race. British Rule was often maintained not by military force but by collaboration with the local elites. White officials would try to incorporate the local rulers into the ceremonial and honours system of home. Many images survive of Indian princes festooned in the medals and ribbons of the English Court.

Whilst this system affected all of Britain's colonies it is important to note that an overall hierarchy existed which graded the numerous colonies. Thus the first four great areas of settlement America, Canada, South Africa and Australia were regarded as more advanced, more civilised, these were followed by India and somewhere near the bottom of the heap Africa. These views informed Britain's attitudes towards all countries even in Europe. Spain's relative economic weakness and decline in imperial ambition placed it firmly as a second-class nation. Ireland was thought of similarly as was Portugal.

The more powerful European countries were not to be excluded from trying to emulate or even thwart Britain's imperial ambitions. Russia disputed Britain's claim to areas in the Pacific and around the Black Sea. France fought with

Britain over Egypt. After 1870 a united Germany entered the game to be followed by Italy, Belgium and even the USA, a form of "annexation madness" overtook most foreign policies. In spite of rivalry the Europeans would usually act in concert if a colony dare challenge the imperial rule. In 1857 European sympathies were with the British not the Indian Mutineers. In 1900 a united military action put down the Boxer Rebellion in China.

Imperialism brought with massive opportunities for trade and wealth and later huge problems associated with independence. Most of which is beyond the scope of this book. Suffice it to say imperialism indelibly printed on everyone's mind a system of class and racial superiority. It also reinforced the prejudices and stereotypes. We have noted the hierarchy of countries, attitudes towards Africa were greatly formed by the slave trade and inevitably those people taken to the West Indies were considered racially inferior and of the lowest class. Stereotypes developed over previous centuries were reinforced, the Black population were particularly seen as heathens, savages, indolent, immoral and stupid.

The emphasis on indolence for example took no account of the physical conditions in the tropics so inimical to Whites. Europeans tended to believe that the natural fertility of such regions required no effort to grow food. This in turn supplied a spurious justification for slavery - without the system, the Black would revert to slothfulness. In England Black unemployment was aired to support the natural laziness of the Black population, many simply refused to examine the social origins of the situation.

Evidence of black stupidity was drawn from the lack of achievements deemed worthy by European society. The myth grew out of the European stubbornness to accept that the artistic, philosophic and mechanical arts are not best served by people living in poverty and slavery.

The immorality of the Black, in English eyes, owed much

to the lack of clothing which loomed large in the early reports and impressions given about Africa. Later where, "demographic factors led to patterns of morality which seemed to fit no moral order recognised by the English" (p.61 'Race in Britain'), in other words where slavery in the West Indies had dictated a completely different view of relationships when husbands and wives could be split up, families divided, obviously the social niceties of Victorian Britain were not observed. Stable monogamous relationships were not possible for the basic reason that sexual imbalance and the movement of slaves made such relationships virtually impossible.

Influential writers helped to reinforce these myths, Thomas Carlyle suggested that by working for about thirty minutes a day the Negro could supply all his wants. Edward Lang described slaves as being libidinous and shameless "as monkeys and baboons" (Long's "History of Jamaica" was once seen as a classic analysis of a colonial society). Anthony Trollope, following a West Indian tour on behalf of the Post Office, noted the 'Negro' West Indian was unambitious, idle, sensual, content with little. Even Charles Dickens lent his support to the brutal crushing of the Jamaican Revolt in 1865. By 1884, such an august institution as the Encyclopaedia Britannica claimed: "No full blooded Negro has ever been distinguished as a man of science, a poet or an artist…"

There were even attempts to establish scientific proof of the differences between Black and white. The Anthropological Society in London maintained that behaviour was determined by profiles of colour and shape as well as of class and culture. Thus the primacy of white over yellow over black was asserted. Many alleged experts denied a common ancestry and claimed non whites could never reach white levels of civilisation. In spite of Darwin's theories and discoveries about ethnic mixing, these "Scientific Racist" theories proved extremely difficult to dislodge from the public consciousness.

By the time of Daniel Tull's arrival in Britain a view of society had been established whereby most people viewed a black person as the lowest in the complicated social hierarchy. A view which usually clung to the generations that black equalled idle and promiscuous. Daniel was none of those things, he arrived an educated hard-working and ambitious man. By the time of Walter's birth in 1888, Victoria ruled over a quarter of the globe - but things were changing abroad and at home. Colonial rule was challenged, the Indian Mutiny, the Boer War, the Boxers, the Jamaican Revolt and at home the rights of the working class were being asserted. In the same year as Walter's birth, the women at the Bryant and May match factory had gone on strike against the dangerous conditions in which they worked. The following year saw the London Dockers' strike. The infant union movement was gaining concessions in terms of shorter hours, the minimum ages for employment and improved wages from the previous unchallenged employers. The voice of the working class was being heard for the first time in Parliament with the rise of the Independent Labour Party. The Right to Vote for all men over 21 was finally granted in the late 1880s. The omission of women led to the establishment of the Suffragette Movement.

By the end of the nineteenth century many 'pressure' groups were established to fight for: the young, the poor, the workers, the equality of women, conspicuous by its absence was a group to look after the interests of the Black community. It is easy to see why a government facing such changes would not encourage a liberal view of the Black community - a black and white united working class would have been a formidable 'enemy'.

Given the lack of support and the stereotypical views of the idleness of the Black it is not hard to see why so few black athletes were encouraged and helped to get to the highest level in their chosen sport. As Walter took the first steps in his professional career he had only one example to follow that of Ghanaian Arthur Wharton. Wharton had made the initial breakthrough by a black player into soccer's professional ranks, playing for twenty years, between 1884-1904, appearing for a variety of northern clubs including the famous "Invincibles" Preston North End; amongst other clubs he numbered: Sheffield United, Rotherham Town, Darlington and Stockport County. At the peak of his career as a goalkeeper Wharton was touted as an international prospect but in spite of many excellent performances the call never came, there was no obvious barrier in terms of an established or superior player, in fact during Arthur's best years the FA selected seven other goalkeepers. Was there an unofficial colour ban? What is certain is that it would be another seventy years before a black player represented England in a full international.

By the time of Walter Tull's Spurs debut, Wharton had left the scene leaving Walter as the lone black player in either Football or Southern Leagues. Using the simplest of calculations, the two leagues comprised of sixty teams, the starting line ups alone required 660 players. Walter was one in 660!

In Scotland the situation was very similar, John Walker became the first black player, appearing for Leith Athletic against Hibernian in 1898 (recent research has indicated the possibility of an earlier black player who may also have played for Scotland). He soon moved to Hearts where his popularity allowed him to lose the soubriquet "Walker the Darkey" for the "Black Jewell", sadly his success was short lived and he died prematurely in 1900. Outside the professional ranks in Scotland just as in England there were many black players performing at a senior competitive level, interestingly one such first happened to be Walter's brother Edward who between 1904 and 1912 appeared for Ayr Parkhouse, Girvan Athletic and Ballantrae.

Sadly the nicknames given to these black footballers had nothing to do with their abilities but solely on their colour for example, Walker "the Darkey", elsewhere it is noted that

Walter was referred to in an Arsenal programme as "Darkie Tull". Wharton was often referred to similarly; the Athletic News reported: "The darkey... can give most goalkeepers a good start and a beating." They may have reached the top but they were still patronised and not allowed to forget where they came from.

In other sports the situation was very similar. James Peters born in Manchester, was capped for England at Rugby between 1906-1908, like Walter he was the only black player in a white dominated sport.

Arthur Wharton's name came up again in the world of athletics, his prowess as a sprinter made him a 'superstar' of the late Victorian era. He became the first person to run the hundred yards in under ten seconds, at the Amateur Athletics Championship in 1886 held at Stamford Bridge. As the unofficial world champion he too faced the exclusively white competition. His ability did not protect him from the jealousy of his rivals, Phil Vasili notes in his book "The First Black Footballer" that at one meeting a competitor remarked, "We can beat a bloomin' nigger anytime". Wharton's response was to offer to box his rival, an offer swiftly declined.

No other black athlete made such an impact at the time, no British athlete made an impact at the newly restored Olympic Games. It was not until 1924 when Harold Abrahams became the first ethnic minority Briton to take Olympic Gold in the hundred yards event, in Paris. Abrahams was a Jew and his exploits and problems have been properly explained in the film, "Chariots of Fire". It was left to the Black American Jessie Owens to finally dispel the myth about the inferiority of black athletes and at what better stage and place than the Berlin Olympics of 1936, thus trashing Hitler's infamous racist theories.

Because of its close association with Empire and its exportation to the Indian sub-continent and to the British colonies in Africa and the West Indies, cricket could reasonably have been expected to produce a number of black players, it did at least in theory allow for British subjects to play for England. Once again we can identify the exception rather than the rule, the most notable and successful coloured cricketer of the pre war period was, Prince Kumar Shri Ranjitsinhji. "Ranji" as he was popularly known played for and captained Sussex and represented England in four series against Australia. His best years as a batsman, 1899-1904 saw him twice-top 3,000 runs in a season. Ranjitsinhji was clearly an exception and was able to surmount any obstacle with the combination of wealth, position, talent and university education. Also in terms of his ethnic background, as an Indian he was perceived as being less barbaric and more refined on the scale of ethnicity he was at a more advanced position than anyone of Afro-Caribbean background. By 1907 he had become the Maharaja of Nawaragar and after the First World War became a delegate at the League of Nations.

In strong contrast the next major black figure in English cricket, Learie Constantine, who first came to Britain in 1923 from the West Indies found a very different reception first playing in the Lancashire Leagues and later captaining his country. In 1943, Constantine sued the manageress of the Imperial Hotel, Russell Square for breach of contract, he and his family were refused admission on the grounds, "he was a nigger". He was awarded £5 damages. In later years Constantine like Ranji before him became an important political figure serving latterly as the Trinidad and Tobago High Commissioner to Great Britain.

In looking at the development of cricket in the Caribbean, it was not until the last two decades of the nineteenth century when the black population had an opportunity to participate. In many circles it was felt that there were too few white people on each island to support the game and therefore Blacks were grudgingly allowed to play. In 1893 Barbados and British Guiana were still threatening to pull out of their fixtures with Trinidad if they fielded any of the country's black players. At best the black players were there to make up the numbers, little wonder there were no black Caribbean players plying their trade on the county cricket circuit during Walter's lifetime. Given the countries' attitude towards white professional players and the old Gentlemen and Players division, a combination of Gary Sobers, Viv Richards and Brian Lara would have had trouble getting a game!

Nevertheless the black players quickly picked up the skills of the game and as they improved, the more likelihood there would be some acceptance, sometimes an opening would be found in one of the island's firms. Cricket gradually gave black players an opportunity of feeding the family, finding a job, a passport to a better life.

As good as the black players became, it was believed their captain should be white, a view which held until the late 1950's and early 60's with the emergence of the late, great Frank Worrall. It was this sort of contradiction that Learie Constantine campaigned so bitterly about, acceptance as players but considered incapable of leadership qualities and quite simply their reversion, off the field, to being second class citizens.

Boxing saw more success for black and coloured athletes than in most other sports it also whipped up the most controversy. At the beginning of the nineteenth century, Bill Richmond, a black boxer set up an academy in London. Amongst his protégés was the celebrated American black Tom Molineaux who fought the undefeated English champion Tom Cribb. Molineaux's career is celebrated in George Macdonald Fraser's novel "Black Ajax". At the turn of the century Ted "Kid" Lewis emerged to take British and World Titles. The American Jack Johnson became the first black heavy weight champion of the world. Boxing's brutal side somehow allowed for black participation but would not celebrate its success, Molineaux and Johnson both became hate figures for their lifestyles and for daring to try to equal their white counterparts.

They were the embodiment of everything the white bigots

despised and for many the only way these men could have won was because the Black athlete had an unfair physical advantage. Whites were more evolved and civilised although this did not prevent a frantic search for a white boxer to retake the Crown and put the black man back in his place!

In those areas where blacks were seen to derive unfair physical advantage from their less "civilised" situation, the white response was often to simply get rid of the competition so, for example, in Britain for a period between the two world wars, successful black boxers were not allowed to fight for British titles. In America, in horse racing, black jockeys who dominated the scene were refused new licences to race.

It is hardly surprising given the issues discussed here that Walter fell foul of the Bristol City hooligans (see chapter 4). The historical part Bristol's port played in the slave trade may explain the prejudice. The influence of scientific racism would also play a part. To them, Walter was merely a stereotype although to such crude and foul-mouthed morons, that is a word they would not have used or understood.

Chapter Four

Working in the Home's printing department did nothing to dim Walter's love of football. Too old for the Home's team, he was persuaded by a friend to write to Clapton F.C. for a trial. Clapton at that time was a very successful side reaching the Amateur Cup Final in 1905,1907,1909 and 1915. Furthermore they were a local side, based at the Old Spotted Dog ground in Upton Lane. The unusual name derived from the public house which stood beside the pitch. Originally a cricket ground it was soon converted to soccer with two large wooden stands running down each touchline.

Walter's application proved successful and he was invited for training and appeared in several trial matches for Clapton's 'A' team. Training on mid week evenings fitted conveniently with his job as a printer and gradually Walter's name was noticed in the local press. It appeared in the "Stratford Express" in October 1908 for scoring two goals in the 'A' team's 3-2 win over Borough Road College. A month later the same paper noted a fine performance against Woodford Albion.

A series of convincing performances finally gave him an opportunity in the first team. The "Express" listed the team for Clapton's Isthmian League match against Nunhead (in later years Denis Compton began his football career with Nunhead) in December 1908 and noted Walter's inclusion at centre forward, justified because "...he had been playing so well for the'A' team."

Breaking into the first eleven was no mean feat; Clapton already had players such as Charlie Rance who like Walter would soon turn professional for Tottenham Hotspur. Another fine player was Clive Purnell, he had been part of the Great Britain side that won the gold medal at the 1908 Olympics.

Walter's first game proved successful as Nunhead were easily defeated and he retained his place for the rest of the season. One of his next games came in the first round of the

Amateur Cup. Clapton were drawn at home to close neighbours, Newportonians. Their opponents were a team formed by old boys of the Newport Road School in Leyton. The old boys were easily defeated in front of a four figure crowd by four goals to nil. Clapton's gates were often measured in thousands, especially for cup ties, as good as this was for the club's bank balance- none came close to the record 12,000 for an F.A. Cup tie versus Spurs in 1898.

The second round of the cup saw an away tie against Great Yarmouth Town. A goal by Rance was enough to guarantee a home draw against Tufnell Park who had disposed of London Caledonians and Oxford City in previous rounds. Tufnell provided Clapton with a comfortable 5-1 victory and Walter although credited with an assist for one of the goals, was guilty of missing an easy chance in the last five minutes.

The quarter finals promised a much stiffer task with strong sides such as Dulwich Hamlet, Bromley, Atherstone and Leytonstone still left in the competition. Clapton faced a tough draw away to local rivals Leytonstone. The match was played in front of a very healthy 2,000 spectators and few watching could have guessed at what would happen. From the kick off Clapton dictated the play with Walter prominent in all the attacking moves. Playing deep one moment and as an out and out striker the next, it seemed as though he had anticipated the role of Hidgekuti, the deep lying Hungarian forward of the famous Magyars of the 1950's. It was no surprise Walter was considered the man of the match, creating four of the goals and scoring two in an incredible 8-1 rout .It was certainly the performance of the round if not of the whole season. It was the largest winning margin in that year's competition, although the 4th Battalion King's Royal Rifles had scored nine times against Ware in round one, Ware replied with four goals. The highest ever scores in the competition to that date belonged to South Bank and Rushden who both totaled twelve goals in home ties. Rushden would become a much more significant feature in Walter's later life when he moved to the Northamptonshire town shortly after joining Northampton Town F.C.

The draw for the semi finals was eagerly awaited. The three other surviving teams were Atherstone, who had put in a very smart performance of their own in defeating Barking 6-1 in the quarter finals, Eston United from near Middlesborough and Dulwich Hamlet. The draw paired Clapton and Atherstone, Eston and Dulwich. Fortuitously Clapton's game would be played at nearby Ilford's Newbury Park. Poor Dulwich faced the long journey to the north east and Darlington FC's ground.

Clapton's strike force of centre forward Rance, inside right Purnell and inside left Tull were targeted by the Atherstone team as the barrier between them and their first final. Sadly for Atherstone's defence it was to no avail as all three scored a goal and Clapton were into the final for the third time in five years. The first final in 1905 saw defeat to West Hartlepool by three goals to two. The next appearance- 1907 saw Stockton defeated at Stamford Bridge by two goals to one.

Clapton's opponents in the final were Eston United, they had squeezed past Dulwich in a very tight game, 2-1. The final would be played at Newbury Park thus giving Clapton something of an advantage. The date for the game was 17th April 1909 just eleven days before Walter's twenty first birthday. It had been a rapid rise for the young printer stepping from impromptu games at the Home to the final of the prestigious Amateur Cup Final. Newbury Park was to prove something of a lucky ground for Walter as a month earlier he scored two goals in a 3-1 victory over Bromley to put Clapton into the final of the London Senior Cup.

Whatever nerves the young man had can only be guessed as he lined up for the kick off. Five thousand people, certainly the largest crowd Walter had played before, were in attendance. The gabled grandstand was packed including several members of his family. The large open ground and wide terraces provided a suitable backdrop for the most important game in Walter's fledgling career. In another curious link, Clapton had been Ilford's first opponents when Newbury Park opened, it seemed like a good omen. In later years the final would be played in more august premises although it was not until 1949 when Wembley hosted its first final Bromley beating Romford 1-0 in front of a staggering 94,000 people.

The final proved to be anticlimactic, the "Athletic News" headlined "Clapton's Easy Triumph". Early goals by Attwood and Purnell put Clapton comfortably in the driving seat. Purnell's goal was laid on after "clever work by Tull". Walter was unlucky to hit a post with a powerful drive from the edge of the area. At half time the score remained 2-0. Eston's hopes of a revival were soon destroyed as they had a player sent off and Charlie Rance scored a hat trick, Walter providing the pass for his third goal. Purnell ended the rout with, "one of his old time lightning drives." The inside trio had come up with the goods again. The cup was presented by Colonel Griffiths of the Kent F.A. and after some well merited celebration of the club's second success in the final. The trophy was placed on display in the surgery window of Dr. Cheetham, on the Romford Road; Dr. Cheetham being a prominent vice president of the Clapton club.

For the record the teams on that auspicious day were:

Clapton :-

Jackson

Bayley Duce

Parkinson Rist Olley

Attwood Purnell Rance Tull Harvey

Eston :-

Hollis Ellis Best Cail Smith

Bunn Housham Callaghan

Bell Vintner

Harrison

Having won the pre-eminent trophy available to teams of their standing, Clapton also won the London Senior Cup that season. A closely contested league saw them in fifth place with twenty points from eighteen games, only three points behind champions Bromley. 1908-09 could arguably be claimed to be the club's best ever season. Such success did not go unnoticed and professional clubs were looking closely at Walter and centre forward Rance. Most particularly scouts from Tottenham had been tracking Walter for several weeks, they were particularly keen to find a replacement for Vivien Woodward who was about to retire. Woodward, a stalwart of the Olympic team may even have been informed of Walter by their team mate Clive Purnell. However, " the catch of the season", with over twenty league and cup goals in his debut season was on his way and when the "Stratford Express" previewed the coming season 1909-10 early in September, it noted with some economy that, "Tull, the West Indian centre forward, has signed on for Tottenham Hotspur."

Spurs had not been the only team interested in signing Walter, there had been offers from several clubs including several unspecified Midlands clubs which may have included Leicester and Derby. Nevertheless Spurs won the day, their confidence in Walter probably bolstered by using him as an amateur in a few fixtures for their 'A' and reserve teams before the end of the season. One of these games happened to be in the final of the London Professional Charity Cup; an amazing season for the young player, three winners' medals and a professional contract.

Signing as a professional caused Walter some heartache, it was difficult for him to reconcile his Methodist upbringing with the morality of accepting wages for playing sport. He wrote to Mr. Morgan at Bonner Road, "I expect you were very disappointed when you heard that I had signed professional forms of the Tottenham Football Club. But I fully intended when I said goodbye to you to remain an Amateur. If I had gone to the Midlands as I said I should have been a "paid" amateur which in my opinion is far worse than taking wages." Walter had earlier hinted of an approach, made by an unspecified Midland League club, about him playing as an amateur. The club being prepared to pay him via the traditional brown envelope left in the changing room. Nevertheless economic considerations won the day, as poor as the wages might seem against today's nonsensical payments a footballer could earn more than a printer! Walter received a £10 signing on fee and although the exact terms of his weekly wages are not known it could not have been more than £4 per week, the maximum wage under restrictions imposed by the Football League in May, 1900; wages would be reduced accordingly in the close season to say £2 or £3. The maximum wage would remain until 1961, when it reached a peak of twenty pounds. Things had not changed a great deal by the 1950's when Jimmy Greaves noted that when he first signed for Chelsea he was paid £8 in the winter and £7 in the summer. A paltry enough sum for a future England international who scored 44 times in 57 appearances for his country.

Given the reported minimum wage needed to maintain a family was estimated to be £1.25 a week and the National Insurance Act of 1911 applied to those earning less than £1.60, then Walter was clearly amongst the better paid workers. There must have been a matter of pride at stake as well, Clapton as successful as they were could not hold a candle to Spurs, newly promoted and at the time the premier club in the south of England, with a fine ground to match.

Walter may have played only a short time for Clapton, his meteoric rise continued at Spurs. Within a few weeks he was on the boat to South America to tour Argentina and Uruguay with the first team. Spurs were joined on the trip by fellow first division side Everton. Certainly touring was not unheard of but such a tour as this must have been beyond Walter's wildest dreams. He did, however, come down to earth with a bump suffering badly on the voyage out from sea sickness and sunstroke. He again wrote to Mr. Morgan, "The heat for the last week or so has been awful I think I had just a touch of sunstroke and felt very queer for a few days. "[13]

Football in Argentina and Uruguay had begun under the auspices of ex pat Britons. In 1893 the first Argentine league was created, the original twenty clubs being British under the watchful president A.Watson- Hutton, headmaster of the well to do St.Andrews Scottish School. During the early years of the twentieth century the dominant team was the Alumni Football Club created by students of the Buenos Aires High School. The popularity of soccer quickly spread to the local population and by the time of the Spurs' tour there were several regional leagues and an established international fixture between the two South American countries for the Lipton Trophy. The trophy donated by Sir Thomas Lipton of tea fame, was the result of his visit to Argentine looking for land to establish tea plantations.

The three week tour began in Montevideo and a one sided 8-0 romp against the Uruguay league. Two days later the first of two exhibition games between the English league sides was played on June 5th in Palermo and ended 2-2. The local paper, "The Standard", reported the next day that, "There is no doubt that the game was a good one and some of the short passing was delightful to watch."

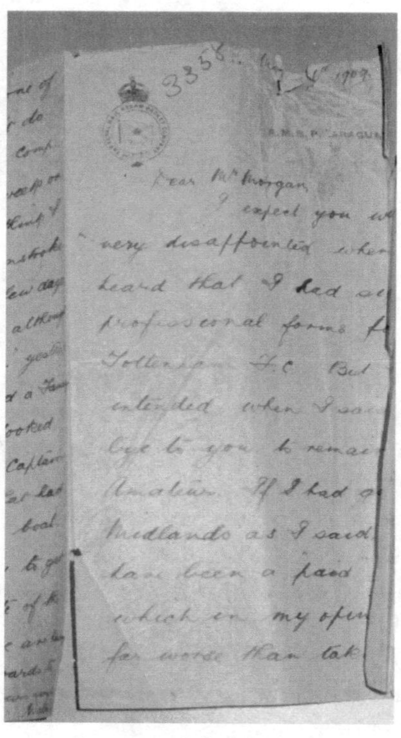
R.M.S.P. "ARAGUA"

Dear Mr Morgan,
I expect you w
very disappointed when
heard that I had s
professional forms f
Tottenham F.C. But
intended when I sa
bye to you to remai
Amateur. If I had
Midlands as I said
have been a paid
which in my opin
far worse than tak

Letter to Mr Morgan

13 NCH Archive

Walter did not play in these opening fixtures but there was plenty of scope for him later in a busy tour.

The third fixture also played in Palermo pitched Spurs against Argentinos, a side composed entirely of players born in the country. Without the English ex pats little was expected but Spurs were in for a shock against some extremely robust tackling and a particularly tight defence. Spurs squeaked through thanks to a solitary goal from McConnor. This would be McConnor's second goal and second but last match for Spurs. The local press was ecstatic about the result and interest in Spurs and Everton took a dramatic rise, Everton had also struggled to beat Argentinos 4-2. Three days later a capacity crowd filled the Palermo Stadium hoping to see a real upset as a potentially stronger Liga Argentine side lined up against Spurs. Once again the local side resorted to rough house tactics but to little avail as goals from Bull, Minter, Clark and McFarlane gave them a comfortable 4-1 victory.

Walter appeared at centre forward and received his fair share of abuse. Although no name is mentioned it appears a Spurs player was sent off for retaliation but re-instated on appeal by the club officials. The mind boggles what would have happened had Rattin in 1966 or David Beckham in 1998 had their cards rescinded!

The busy tour was concluded over the next five days with the second game against Everton played in Palermo. Everton won 4-0 possibly aided by the knocks and injuries suffered by the Spurs' players in their two previous games. Order was restored on the 20th June as Spurs crushed Rosario 9-0 and a few days later the premier club side Alumni easily beaten by four goals to nil.

Just for good measure on the 23rd June many of the Spurs players including Walter attended a fixture between two local sides. Reports suggest that a bigger crowd than usual turned up with the result being a minor pitch invasion as people jostled to see; although nothing to Spurs who had seen this sort of infringement many times, they were shocked however to see how the problem was solved. Several members of the Argentinian cavalry raced onto the pitch and set about the spectators with the flats of their swords. Needless to say order was quickly restored and no-one felt the necessity to stray onto the pitch again. Just for the record Phil Vasili has written a screenplay of the tour and several scenes including the pitch invasion can be found on his web site.

After the Alumni game the touring teams boarded ship to return to England, according to letters sent home by Walter he suffered no repeat of the sea-sickness and the journey proved particularly enjoyable featuring amongst other entertainments a fancy dress contest. Both voyages proved very enjoyable for on the way out, when not seasick, Walter wrote about "crossing the line" and enjoying another Fancy Dress Ball. The success of the celebration prompted the Captain to claim it had been the "best ever held on this boat". In spite of the adventure and the parties Walter was missing England; again he wrote to Morgan, "I shall be very glad to get home again, in spite of the interesting voyage we are having".

It was thus a happy Spurs team that left South America to face their inaugural season in division one. Walter obviously had impressed sufficiently to be selected for the opening game away to Sunderland. But it was an unhappy Spurs team that returned to London from the north east on the back of a 1-3 defeat. Disappointed he may have been by that result but Walter, in a few months of his debut for Clapton, was now a first division footballer with the biggest club in the south and an exotic foreign tour under his belt, it was something of an achievement!

The fairy story continued for Walter with the visit of Manchester United, a glamorous team even then, to open Spurs' first division home campaign. There was a double first as the game saw the official opening of the remodelled White Hart Lane, the new stand described by the " Athletic News" as, "The greatest and best appointed grandstand in England." A large crowd of 35,000 waited in eager anticipation.

Walter Tull of Tottenham Hotspur F.C.
The picture is signed and dated 17th January 1911

The home fans were somewhat frustrated as the previous season's cup holders took an early lead and then had what appeared to be a perfectly good goal disallowed. After a lively five minutes Walter made his presence felt as, "Tull, in manoeuvring for position carried the ball to the extreme corner of the penalty area. Roberts tore across to intercept him, and throwing both feet at the ball he succeeded in turning it over the line, but brought Tull to the ground at the same moment." (Athletic News) A penalty was given and scored by Steel. The report also noted the United keeper Mage saving "hot shots" from Minter and Tull. The game ended as a 2-2 draw, Spurs' second goal also a penalty.

The "Daily Chronicle" was effusive in its praise of Walter, complimenting his "coolness", plying the wingers with perfect passes, emphasizing his footwork. Where it was noted that previously critics had charged him with being slow the "Chronicle" defended him saying no greater footballer was ever seen to hurry. In a final simple but eloquent summation it acknowledged: "Tull is very good indeed". Even now Walter was not getting carried away by this success, still firmly set in the back of his mind was the idea that if he failed to make it he would return to printing, he still thought he might, "get a place on one of the newspapers if I can't do that I shall work as a comp." On a postcard to his brother, Edward, he reflected on his league debut saying he felt completely exhausted in the second half and was carried by the "noise and commotion" of the Spurs' supporters. He also noted that a draw had, "not flattered the opposition."

The next game saw Walter's first goal for Spurs scored against Bradford City. His joy being somewhat overshadowed by a 5-1 defeat. The first half was particularly poor for both sides and Walter was picked out for particular criticism. However his goal put the score level and "Woolwinder" writing for the "Athletic News" reported, "In the second half Tull displayed such improved form that there was the promise of a close fight and a close finish." Things went slightly awry as the home team scored four quick goals! Just before the end of the game Walter received a knock that would keep him out of the team for the next game. He returned on the 9th of October to face Bristol City; a game that would prove harrowing in the extreme.

City were a useful side, as mentioned they narrowly lost in the previous season's cup final. They had been promoted in the 1905-6 season as second division champions with Manchester Utd. as runners up. In the next three seasons they had finished 2nd, 8th and 10th. Prior to winning promotion they achieved the unique distinction of finishing 4th in three consecutive seasons, each time with the same number of points, 42! Thus the Spurs side could have expected a rough ride in Bristol.

What they did not expect was the abuse and racial taunting dished out by a substantial minority of the crowd to Walter. Undoubtedly Walter suffered some abuse as a youngster and whilst playing amateur football. Even amateurs are not choirboys, certainly it would not be left to the professionals to try to put a player off his game by insulting his race, colour, creed or questioning his parentage. But the Bristol crowd took it beyond such limits with their systematic and cruel jibes. It says much for Walter's dignity that at no time did he react to such provocation. This incident clearly brings to mind the similar treatment meted out to John Barnes, Cyrille Regis, Laurie Cunningham, Brendan Batson, all of whom recall the abuse and bananas thrown from the stands. Batson recalls early games for WBA when: “We were still greeted at games by monkey chants and bananas”. As appalling as this behaviour was Batson and co. could at least take some comfort from the thought that they were not alone, sadly Walter was.

For once Walter's accelerated progress from orphanage star to the peak of the amateur game to the peak of the professional seems to have stalled; the effects of the, “language lower than Billingsgate”, to quote the reporter for the "Football Star" must have devastated Walter. His confidence took a severe jolt. Whatever else, Walter was a humble and fair man this irrational treatment must have shaken him to the core. Walter did play in Spurs' next two games without making much of an impression. A close 1-0 win over Bury described as having an "abnormally low level of play" by the Athletic News and an away game at Middlesborough, where his lack of pace was commented on. In a remarkable piece of reporting Walter was referred to as, "The Folkestone foreigner the dusky Tull."

Walter appeared for the rest of the season playing second team football; it is hard to assume that he did not warrant being picked again. Stung he may have been but Tull was a strong and Christian man he would not have allowed himself to be down for long. Phil Vasili suggests the long sojourn in the reserves may have had a lot to do with the directors being unwilling to face up to potential further trouble embarrassing an ambitious and new club in the league. If this were so then those directly involved would carry a heavy burden of guilt, not least for frustrating the personal ambitions of a talented player but in the longer term re-inforcing the stereotype of the Bristol thugs' invention.

Fortunately for Walter there were lighter moments in the season. Although he played in only a handful of league matches, he did have the opportunity of playing in the London Charity Cup campaign. He featured in the semi-final tie against Queens Park Rangers on a bleak, rainy day in November. Spurs beat the Southern League team 4-1. Strangely in a brief match report, the scorers were omitted but mention is made of the, "skills of the West Indian forward Tull." The final paired Spurs with Fulham in December and the semi-final score was repeated. Sadly this time in Fulham's favour, but at least Walter received a medal for his efforts.

The following season saw no improvement in Walter's personal fortunes, again there was limited scope for his talents in the first team. One game to savour was a close 1-2 defeat away to Manchester City but at least Walter scored the goal. He spent a successful time in the championship winning reserves playing in 27 games and scoring 10 goals. Significantly three of the goals came against Northampton Reserves in a South Eastern League match during February 1911.

In a one sided affair Walter scored three goals as Spurs won 7-1; the "Northampton Football Echo" little realising they would soon be reporting on Tull on a regular basis recorded that, "After eleven minutes Tull scored a pretty goal for Tottenham". This performance must have certainly caught the eye of the Northampton Officials, maybe even Herbert Chapman was in attendance. Whatever else happened Walter Tull was marked as the next transfer target for the Cobblers.

It is worth mentioning here that Northampton's nickname derived from the town's main industry shoe-making and was not a reflection on their play. Although many would argue later this was a very fair reflection during the late 1970's and at other low points.

At least Walter was enjoying success albeit as a member of a highly successful reserve team. His performances that season apart from catching the eye of Herbert Chapman also caught the eye of the league officials who selected him for their representative side who played against Chelsea at the end of the season.

Meanwhile Spurs' first eleven were struggling badly having lost 3-0 away to Notts. County on March 12th, they recorded only two more victories in the next six weeks. Walter's good form for the reserves was ignored. Injury eventually allowed for Walter's "swansong" for the first team on 8th April at the Manor Ground, Plumstead - Arsenal's home ground. It seems somehow fitting that Walter's final game should be against Spurs bitterest rivals and played before Arsenal's largest crowd that season 24,853.

Walter played because Percy Humphreys was injured, Humphreys had gained one cap for England against Scotland in a 1-2 defeat. Humphreys was a hard act to follow for Walter, for in just under two years Humphreys had been at Spurs he had scored 29 goals in 50 games, here is another strong reason why Walter's first team chances were limited. The "Weekly Herald", see below, was certain about who was better value. The teams that day were:

Arsenal: Burdett, Shaw, Gray, Ducat, Sands, McEarchrane, Greenaway, Common, Chalmers, Hoare and Lewis.

Spurs: Lunn, Collins Wilkes, Bentley, Rance, Darnell, Curtis, Minter, Tull, Steel and Middlemiss.

Not for the first or indeed the last time Tull pulled on the number 9 jersey. In the opposing side, was amongst the other luminaries, Alf Common the subject of the first four figure transfer fee. Common was also an international winning the last of three caps against Wales in 1906.

"The Sportsman" picked Common as the man of the match. "Spurs had no brainy forward like Common. The veteran may be slow, but he retains all his intuition for placing a colleague easily. He paved the way to the first goal, scored the second and was as great a source of trouble to Lunn as any attacker."

Whereas to the same reporter Walter was just slow, "...he lacks the important essentials of a centre forward, speed and ability for bustling."

The "Weekly Herald" was even more critical, "The Tottenham front men did not blend well and their work was altogether unconvincing. Passes were so frequently ill-judged or intercepted that there were comparatively few sustained movements. Humphreys with his bustling ways would have been more effective against Sands than Tull, who was too slow and was often beaten."

For the record Spurs lost the game 2-0, Arsenal's goals scored by Common and Chalmers. Just to add insult to injury the match programme recorded Walter as "Darkie Tull"!

Chapter Five

Exchanging Spurs' first division status for the Southern League and Northampton was understandable, Walter was eager for regular first team football, however, swapping London for Northampton in every other respect must have been a culture shock. Northampton was a small town with little to recommend it. It had a large market square, a dozen or so cinemas, an average selection of shops stretching up from the site of the old castle along the inaptly named Gold Street, up the Drapery and heading north into Abington Street, the main thoroughfare, housing the Notre Dame High School. The school's lofty dark walls dominated the New Theatre which stood opposite. The roads were mainly cobbled and that with the tram lines gave pedestrians a very uneasy progress. The town's major claim to fame was in its one industry- shoemaking. Dozens of factories turned out every kind of footwear from elegant ladies' slippers to boots for the military. The boot and shoe industry had existed in the town for centuries and had cost the town its castle and walls. Supporting Parliament during the Civil War, it provided the Roundheads with excellent footwear; the battle at nearby Naseby signalled the last real chance of victory for Charles I but with the Restoration came restitution. Charles II decreed that as punishment the castle would be razed. Had the monarch waited longer the Great Fire of Northampton (1675) would have probably done the job for him. In an ironic footnote Charles provided huge amounts of timber to rebuild the town all at his own expense!

There was some sporting pedigree in the town, the football club had made great strides in its short history, in ten years from its foundation the club rose from the local Northants' league to the powerful Southern League. The local rugby team, known locally as “The Saints” provided several internationals including Edgar Mobbs, more of whom later. The county cricket eleven elevated to first class status as recently as 1905 shared the County Ground with the footballers. Surprisingly there was a great enthusiasm for cycling which was another sport practiced on the County Ground, one of the pioneers for cycling was Joseph Grose who later owned several large garages in the town. In 1883 he was recorded as achieving the surprising speed of 20mph at the Leicester Cycle Track!

Walter was not entirely exiled in his new town the railway ran regular trains to London, the local newspaper claiming a gentleman could run up to town, work between 10-4 and return to "bosom of his family in time for a fashionable dinner."

Walter signed for the Cobblers on 17th October 1911, the deal involved a double transfer with Charlie Brittan joining Spurs. The loss of Brittan was considered by "Councillor" in the Northampton "Daily Echo" as a "bombshell" and that "Northampton's loss will undoubtedly be Tottenham's gain, as Brittan is a young player, and has not reached the zenith of his fame."

"Councillor" was however quick to applaud Herbert Chapman's coup in bringing Tull to Northampton, "I must congratulate Mr Chapman upon having captured Tull, the clever West Indian forward of the Tottenham club. This step I really believe, is a great stroke of business, as Tull is a great player, and I have no hesitation in saying he will prove a decided acquisition to Northampton's front rank."

Chapman, the Northampton manager, had indeed pulled off quite a coup bringing the player to Northampton as league clubs Leicester Fosse, Aston Villa and Clapton Orient (not to be confused with the Clapton amateur team) were also interested in signing Tull.

The appeal of the three league clubs must have been considerable Villa finishing the previous season as runners up to Manchester United by the odd point. Leicester and Clapton enjoyed varying success in the second division the former in 15th place, the latter 4th behind champions West Bromwich, runners up Bolton and 3rd placed Chelsea. Spurs that year finished a reasonably comfortable 15th in Division One, the same as 1909-10 and coincidently with the same number of points. At one stage before joining Northampton it appeared Walter was on the point of signing for Heanor Town. However, Herbert Chapman got his man and no doubt Walter was happy with the prospect of first team football.

The exact nature of the deal was not disclosed but with cash and Brittan moving to Spurs, the deal must have been considerable at the time. Northampton's record transfer had been Edwin Lloyd Davies' move from Stoke in 1907, the Cobblers had parted with £400 for the Welsh international; remembering that the record transfer stood at £1,000 for Alf Common's move from Sunderland to Middlesborough only two years earlier it was indeed a lot of money.

The two moves perhaps indicate how close the Southern League was to the Football League in playing standards, that two such players as Tull and Davies were prepared to sign for the "lower" league club. It might be argued that Stoke, at least, were suffering money problems having been relegated from the First Division in 1906-7 and were glad of the cash!

The Northampton side Walter joined had some pedigree led by Herbert Chapman who was later to manage Huddersfield and Arsenal to championship successes: three with Huddersfield and two with Arsenal, a third achieved just after his tragic early death. They included on the playing staff the aforementioned Lloyd Davies who won 16 Welsh caps, this in an era when fewer internationals were played. Twelve of the caps were won whilst playing for Northampton and all of them were won against the home countries: England, Scotland and Northern Ireland. It is hard to imagine a "non-league" player winning international honours today - even for Wales.

Another member of the Northampton side was the diminutive Fred Ingram Walden who was universally known as 'Fanny'. He made his debut for the Cobblers in 1909 and scored a hat-trick in one of his early games against Luton. A small man, only 5 feet 2 inches, he was a very skilful player who later, ironically, signed for Spurs, where he won two caps for England (the first in 1914, the second in 1922). Walden was an all rounder who played county cricket for Northamptonshire and later became a first class umpire, but more of Fanny later.

Frank Bradshaw ex-Sheffield Wednesday and scorer of a hat-trick in his one and only international was another quality player. He left however a few weeks after Walter joined, signing for Everton for a hefty £2,000.

Another indication of the closeness between Football and Southern league standards and one Walter would have been aware of was the annual Charity Cup match held between champions of the respective leagues. In 1909 the Cobblers as Southern League Champions, played Newcastle at Stamford Bridge where they lost a close match 0-2. The result was certainly no disgrace as Newcastle had won the First Division with what was then a record 53 points from 38 matches and with another record - 24 wins. This was bettered only by Sunderland before World War I. Of all the sides making a name for themselves during the early part of the twentieth century, teams such as Manchester United, Liverpool, Sheffield Wednesday - Newcastle were perhaps the finest: between 1905 and 1909 they won three championships. Between 1905 and 1911, they had contested five F.A. Cup finals, winning only one, a replay against Barnsley. The majority of the side were internationals men like Billy McCracken (Ireland), Veitch and Rutherford (England).

Two years later a few months before Tull's transfer the two sides met again in the F.A. Cup in Newcastle. The game watched by over 42,000 ended in a 1-1 draw. The lure of a second sizeable gate, persuaded the Northampton committee to sell the ground rights for £900. Even then the Northampton side only lost the second away game by 2 goals to 1. Walter was leaving a first division club but by no means joining a bad one!

Walter made his debut for Northampton on the 21st

October against Watford, the team was:

Thorpe, Hampson, Clipston, Lloyd-Davies, Hampson, Lessons, Manning, Walden, King, Tull, Bradshaw and Freeman.

Lessons usually played as a forward but turned out at centre half, possibly to accommodate Walter who wore the number nine shirt.

The Northampton "Daily Echo" reported that, "Tull had a warm welcome from the crowd when the Cobblers turned out and he had the privilege of kicking off for his new club."

Thus on a wet and gusty day Walter's Northampton career began. He was involved in the early Northampton pressure and was fouled as the "Echo" so quaintly informs us, "just outside the disaster mark". The resulting free kick coming to nothing as Walter was caught offside.

It is always hard playing for a new team and Walter struggled to make an impact on the game. His most significant contribution came with Northampton 2-1 down, Walter fed the ball to Freeman who, "...beating Lockett dashed inwards. Twenty yards out he shot and Webster never had a chance of touching the ball as it crashed into the net." "Boys Own" style reporting but it must have been a very satisfying moment for the newcomer.

Walter could indeed have made the debut more memorable as later the Echo reporter noted, "Tull might have given the Cobblers the lead if he had accepted a chance at 15 yards' range". Then very late in the game, "Tull got in a shot which Webster put over the bar".

Walter's contribution was perhaps not what he wanted but it was hardly insignificant. He kept his place in the side for the next game a week later.

A week later with Tebbott replacing Manning as left-half, the team travelled to New Brompton and in front of 5,000 people won 3-1.

For those who are not sure about the whereabouts of New Brompton, the following season they became Gillingham.

Regardless of name Walter came in for some rough treatment from the opposition taking a heavy kick on the ankle and limping for most of the first half. Today undoubtedly a substitute would have taken his place but in those days there was no such provision and Walter had to soldier on until half time before receiving treatment. The “Echo” reported that in spite of treatment, “the mischief had been done and Tull's pace reduced appreciably.” There must have been some raised eyebrows amongst the readership as Walter was not renowned as a particularly quick player. Fast on his feet he may not have been but a quick thinker he certainly was and the “Echo” acknowledged as much, “...he showed a genuine capacity for leadership, his display being brainy.” That phrase about his capacity for leadership was to have a poignant echo seven years later.

Walter's third game also proved a success, in the home game against Exeter City, the Cobblers won 2-1. It was to be Frank Bradshaw's last game and although he did not realise it at the time it was to be Walter's last game in the first team for several weeks. The “Echo” had picked out both Bradshaw and Walter as being “not so good as their colleagues.” Walter's first three games had proved to be disappointing for Walter who found he could not reproduce the form that had encouraged Chapman to bring him from Spurs. Some sceptics in the crowd thought him too slow for the hustle of Southern League football. Thus in the following game Walter was replaced by Albert 'Spider' Lewis. Lewis proceeded to score four goals in the next three games and thus consigned Walter to a lengthy wait in the reserves.

The next game in which Walter featured was on the 30th December at home to Coventry when he replaced the injured Lewis. This time wearing number ten, Lessons having returned to the number nine shirt after Bradshaw's move. Nevertheless in front of a healthy 10,000 crowd Walter scored the first goal in a 2-1 win. The “Daily Echo” recorded a “bright and interesting game,” one where, “Three fourths of the play had raged within thirty yards of the Coventry goal." Walter's goal was described thus, "In the second half Tull accepted a lovely chance offered by Whittaker, and the home team maintained the upper hand…" The overall assessment of Walter's contribution came as a somewhat muted, "Tull in Lewis' berth did some sound work." The fixture list over this period makes interesting reading, Northampton playing seven games in December, including fixtures on the 23rd, 25th, 26th and 30th. Little wonder gates of only a couple of thousand attended some of the fixtures during the festive season. The previous year was no better with games on the 24th, 26th, 27th, 28th! Some people say there's too much football today, it makes Sky TV's efforts look quite puny!

During February Walter was selected as travelling reserve for an F.A. cup second round tie, away to Darlington. The team travelled up the day before and spent the night at Seaburn. The weather was foul and the majority of the players found the windows of their rooms frozen so hard they could not close them! In spite of the freezing rooms the game ended 1-1. With Walter again a reserve, the home tie won by 2 goals to nil, Walter's rivals Lessons and King scoring.

Walter did feature in the two following games as a replacement for Freeman and Lewis respectively. The first game was lost 0-2 at Plymouth and the second a sound 7-0 victory over Reading, when Walter recorded his third goal. Unfortunately for Walter he could not convince Chapman of his value and once again found himself in the reserves and this pattern continued to the end of the season with Walter filling in when a forward was injured.

He played a further three games at the end of March and beginning of April missed two and returned with a vengeance playing a further three games and scoring six goals. Against the background of disruption of being in one week and out the next Walter somehow managed to produce one of his most memorable games and surely one of the most satisfying for a number of reasons.

On 13th April, a depleted Northampton side were at home to Bristol Rovers. So short were the team that an injured Lloyd-Davies was forced to play. The very mention of the name Bristol must have sent shivers of revulsion up Walter's spine. Memories of his treatment playing there for Spurs would have been impossible to put aside. One can only imagine his satisfaction scoring four goals - a 5-0 rout, albeit not of City but Rovers, and showing the good citizens of Bristol that they had not crushed him with their unmerciful racial abuse.

It is worth noting that Walter even set up the first goal for Lewis and could have scored more himself as the "Echo" reported several other chances falling to him: "...Freeman got in a sparkling centre, with Tull, Lewis and Redhead all in a bunch. Each one could have taken the ball on the run, and it was left to the centre forward to collar it in his stride and put yards over."

One cannot help but admire such silky prose, the 'sparkling' centre, the collaring of the ball and even Inspector Morse would have appreciated the use of the "Oxford Comma".

Walter's best goal gave him his hat-trick: "Redhead placed forward to Tull and the centre forward beat Roney with a tremendous drive taken with beautiful accuracy."

One could imagine that like Devon Malcolm in the final test of 1994 South African Tour, Walter's pride had been injured and now it was pay back time. One does of course imagine that any words Walter may have had on the matter would have been slightly more eloquent than Devon's immortal lines: "You guys are history". I have deliberately omitted a significant adjective!

It appeared that belatedly Walter might have established himself playing the next two games he scored in a 1-1 draw away to Swindon. Two days later he scored again in a comprehensive 4-0 defeat of Southampton apart from noting Walter's goal, the "Echo" flatly completed its report with the line "Freeman was right off and Tull was rather slow." Typical of such an in and out season Walter was injured for the final game of the season against Luton.

Thus ended what must have been a very frustrating first season at the County Ground although on paper at least 9 goals from 12 games looks very impressive and stands examination against Lewis' 9 goals from 29 games and Freeman's 10 from 35. The two top scorers King and Lessons scored 19 apiece all of which meant that the Northampton forward line was in very good nick and in scoring 82 goals in 38 games were the top scorers in the Southern League. It did look as though Walter was something of a lucky omen for the team. Of the twelve games he played: eight were won and two drawn, a healthy 28 goals scored against 11 conceded. On a personal basis he must have considered whether the next season would bring more opportunities; despite his late flourish, he appeared to be low in the forwards' "pecking order."

The team finished 3rd in the league and only two points adrift of the Champions QPR and with a vastly superior goal average. The home game had seen the Cobblers hammer the Champions 5-1, a game Walter did not feature in. The crucial result was an away 1-2 defeat at QPR, the game before Walter returned to the side against Millwall. Had the away result ended a 1-1 draw Plymouth and Northampton would have tied with QPR and the mathematicians would have had to decide the winner. If, as ever, is a mighty big word. Another if might well have been what if Walter had joined one of the other clubs interested in him - a question he must, almost certainly, have asked himself.

No matter what fortune brought him on the field, Walter had settled happily to life in the country where the locals adopted him as one of their own.

Shortly after joining the Cobblers Walter moved to the nearby town of Rushden to lodge with team mate Eric Tomkins. Rushden, a small market town of some five thousand people relied as did Northampton on the boot and shoe industry. It lacked the factories of the larger town, much of the production was completed by outworkers who adapted part of the many small terraced houses into makeshift workshops. The individual parts being assembled in the actual factory. Some of that industry survives today but Rushden is perhaps better known as being the birthplace of author H.E.Bates and for the meteoric rise in the 1990s of the local football club, Rushden and Diamonds.

In 1911 Walter would have found an intimate atmosphere, a place where everyone knew each other and each others' business. There were a few amenities such as the Palace Theatre which had opened in September 1910. National celebrities and touring shows appeared there frequently and in 1912 Charlie Chaplin appeared there. Films were also shown at the Palace and one film in particular, "The Battle of Waterloo" (1913) proved very popular, as some filming had been done in neighbouring Irthlingborough, many locals had been involved as extras. It would be nice to think of Walter fighting for the Iron Duke. Perhaps a safe bet would be to assume he at least saw the film.

In the company of Eric Tomkins or "Wassie" as he was known locally, Walter discovered plenty of uses for his spare time. Wassie for all of his owlish looks and serious demeanour was a talented, sporting all rounder he played cricket for the town's club in the tough Northamptonshire County League and also represented Northants in the County Championship on 13 occasions, top scoring with an unbeaten half century. He also represented Rushden Thursday first X1. In addition to this he played hockey to county standard, he was thus the only sportsman to be "capped" in three sports by Northamptonshire. For good measure he had represented England Schoolboys in the first ever schoolboy international, a game in which England beat Wales 3-2.

Wassie introduced Walter to his local cricket clubs, where it appears Walter was not an untalented all rounder. The local weekly paper records many of his performances. In June 1913 it notes that Walter took four wickets in a drawn county league game against Bedford. Later in a match against Burton Latimer he scored 22 whilst Tomkins recorded 47 in a total of 141, the game won by 55 runs. Another game against local rivals Rothwell showed Walter taking three wickets and "performing admirably in the field." For the Thursday X1 he opened the bowling and batted at number five, sandwiched between adverts for second hand pianos and a notice about the appointment of school managers, the "Rushden Echo" briefly reported the game between Rushden Thursdays and Bedford Beagley's, "Yesterday at Rushden ending in a draw, Tull took 4 Bedford wickets for 58 and George 2 for 30" The score card showed Walter being caught out for just 1 run in Rushden's 63-6 chasing 132.

Another team Wassie and Walter graced was the Northampton footballers' cricket eleven. There were infrequent but closely fought games against other sides, including Spurs, for whom Herbert Chapman had played in the past. The games were generally played for local charities and certainly the local hospital benefited from these fixtures.

Wassie also encouraged Walter to enjoy the other diversions Rushden offered: musical evenings were regularly provided by the various church groups, amateur dramatics and many other assorted charity events. Walter would not have been unaware of the efforts of his new neighbours when on the 3rd May 1912 a musical evening was staged at the Palace Theatre on behalf of the sufferers as a result of the Titanic's tragic loss. Over £43 was raised by the Rushden residents, "Rushden's Splendid Response" claimed the "Echo". With the football season tucked up the week before it is highly likely that Walter attended the charity event. Walter had in fact appeared for the Cobblers in an earlier charity match against Kettering for the same cause. A worthy £59 was realized in the 1-4 defeat at the hands of Kettering Town. Walter alongside Clipston, Lessons and Freeman were among the most experienced Cobblers' players.

Walter found Eric extremely good company, he was fond of Eric's easy humour and his fondness for card tricks. The two of them found a comfortable understanding which would be reflected often on the football field as they both shared the half back positions for Northampton in nearly 100 games. Even so sharing with Eric and his parents had only been seen as a temporary situation and is was around the middle of 1912 that Walter found other lodgings in the town., moving the short distance to Queen Street, a row of houses leading uphill from the High Street. These dwellings look little different today neat, small houses with the typical long, narrow gardens so common in and around Northants; the only acknowledgments to the new Millennium being a rash of satellite dishes and the complete inability to shoehorn a bicycle between the masses of parked cars.

Queen Street, Rushden

A pre-war view of Queen Street, Rushden, Northamptonshire
Walter lived at number 26, Queen Street from mid 1912
until his death

Chapter Six

At the end of the 1911-12 season Herbert Chapman left Northampton to become manager of Leeds City. In a farewell tribute the local "Northampton Independent" newspaper said that Chapman was, "a fine judge of player, a skilled diplomatist" and that his, "tact and cheery optimism has resulted in his getting the best out of the men at his command."

The new manager at Northampton was Walter Bull who had been touted as manager before Chapman's arrival. Bull was an ex Spurs player and knew Chapman from their playing days, more importantly he knew Walter Tull. Bull was at Spurs when Walter signed for them, he left to join Heanor in June 1910-it was Bull's presence that had prompted Heanor's interest in Walter when he left Spurs. Between then and taking the Cobblers' job he also coached in Argentina.

The season opened with a 2-2 draw away to Southampton, a game which Walter Tull missed, crucially centre-half Hampson was injured. Walter was drafted into the side at centre-half for the game against Gillingham which was won 2-1, with goals from Lloyd-Davies and Lewis but Tull was not considered a success. Over the course of the next three games Bull himself, Rawlings and Lessons were used until Hampson was fit again.

It appeared that Walter would be in for another frustrating season as he played a game at Stoke and was dropped again, on this occasion he was given the centre forward's position and the team lost 0-1. Stoke themselves were going through an equally frustrating period having lost league status two years before they were destined to finish bottom of the Southern League three points adrift of Brentford.

Walter returned for the fixture against Milwall and held his place for the next ten games before receiving an injury playing against Crystal Palace. He left the field after twenty minutes but returned five minutes later. The injury forced him out of the next five games including the incredible 9-0 defeat of Stoke.The game after this Walter was again missing but was probably relieved to be so, as the Cobblers travelled to Blackburn Rovers for an F.A. Cup tie. They returned, somewhat chastened, having suffered a 2-7 reverse. Eighteen goals in two games, Northampton supporters were certainly getting value for money!

It had been suggested that Walter might return for the cup game. He travelled with the team and stayed overnight at St Anne's on Sea on the Friday evening, but on Saturday it was decided not to risk Walter, "...seeing that he has had no obvious test since his accident." Therefore Manning took the right half spot against his old club.

Chastened by a 7-2 walloping the team may have been but disgraced they were not. The Blackburn team had won the league the previous year and would do so again the next season. As for this year they finished a respectable fifth. The Blackburn side was full of international players, men like Bob Crompton who played for England 41 times, as well as 538 league games during an incredibly successful career. He was at the time England's most capped player and on retirement ran a plumber's business and later became a director of Blackburn. In many ways Tom Finney's later career at Preston ran parallel to Crompton's. A last word on Crompton must go to Bryon Butler, who in his official history of the league records that Crompton, "was a full back who was strong enough to have kicked any winger over any stand, but that was not his way. He was a marvellous craftsman, cool, perceptive and scrupulously fair."

Meanwhile, someone at the club, maybe Bull or Harry Burrows the trainer decided that Walter should be tried at wing-half, a position more suited to his style of play. It had already been noted, especially among the supporters that Walter was a little slow for a forward. In this new role Walter appeared against Millwall on the 5th October, the experiment was considered a success on the back of a 1-0 victory. Walter remained at wing-half for the next ten games, his longest consecutive run of appearances thus far. Although personally a success for Walter the team's form remained patchy with four wins, two draws and four defeats.

As noted Walter missed two of the side's more dramatic results as well as four other games. He returned to the team in late January in the away game against Brentford, a dull 0-0 draw against a team low in the table. Walter remained in the side for the remaining fifteen games of the season, moving briefly to the number seven shirt after Fanny Walden's move to Spurs.

Walter's brief appearance in the number 7 shirt was a stop gap measure until a regular replacement could be found for Walden. Nevertheless Walter's first appearance against Coventry (he made 4 further appearances as a winger) was to be unforgettable.

A wet, late Saturday in March promised little a meagre crowd of 2,000 and both sides comfortably in mid table. Tapper in the Northampton “Daily Echo” sets the scene:

"A storm in the morning, and rain until half-past three, on one of the poorest draining grounds in the South, made it a defenders' Bannockburn at one end, while the other was left so that forwards and backs were on a fairly equal - if always unsafe footing."

The martial metaphor may have left readers slightly uncertain but clearly the Coventry forwards had no doubt about exploiting the end advantageous to them. By half time despite Walter's early threats: "Two centres were excellently placed by Tull," "The Cobblers attacked hotly ...but lovely work by Jaques prevented Tull's centre reaching the inside men" ...Coventry led 4-0!

Whatever the half time talk consisted or what was put in the tea the Cobblers clearly had not given up - the conditions were now firmly in their favour and after eight minutes Walter's centre was converted by King. King scored a second and with only 12 minutes remaining earned his hat-trick. Even then it looked as though Coventry might hang on but with seconds to go Walter cleverly linked with Freeman but let's leave the finale to the words of the immortal Tapper:

"The precision of Northampton's methods - the whole team played as one man, was something beautiful to witness. And the last goal! Over to Freeman came the ball from Tull. A few twists in and out, the defence was drawn, and Freeman had transferred to King a dozen yards out, and King crashed the ball forward. It struck the post - such a yell. Two players slipped and fell in the mud; in the excitement no-one gave them a second thought, and I could not tell you who they were. There was a surging wave of struggling forms, and the ball was at the feet of Robert Hughes; two feet of goal left vacant, half a lake and a sodden ball. There would have been every excuse for a slip. But Hughes made no slip. Directly the ball went back to the centre of the field. Referee Shallcross blew his whistle. Fifteen seconds less would have meant the goal would have come too late!"

Mid table yes, boring certainly not; a game that everyone watching or playing would not forget in a hurry. A game which also showed Walter's versatility, he certainly had a very effective game and as noted replaced Walden for the remaining games of the season. Not bad for a player with no pace.

Although as Frank Grande says in his "Official Centenary History" the team had a settled look about it, "for Thorpe kept goal, with Fred Clipstone and captain, Edwin Lloyd-Davies as full backs; Walter Tull, "Jock" Manning and Eric Tompkins made up the half back line, and Walden and local boy Freeman made up the right wing, with Hughes and Smith on the left; free scoring Harry King was at centre forward." For all this stability the team slipped from third the previous season to tenth. Plymouth won the league with 50 points, it's interesting to note Northampton in the previous season finished third with 51.

Walter's satisfaction at having established himself in the team, he made 28 appearances, must have been a little tarnished by the team's modest finish.

Chapter Seven

Walter Bull left the club half way through the 1912-13 season and at least ended any further identification confusion with the subject of this story. The Cobblers were managed for the remainder of the season by committee.

The other major changes involved Fanny Walden signing for Spurs. Before this move Herbert Chapman had tried to sign Walden for Leeds, the approach not revealed to Fanny was countered by the club's arrangement of a “Shilling Fund” which raised over £650 and thus avoided the smaller clubs age old lament of selling their star assets to survive. However, in a splendid departure from logic Walden was shortly after sold to Spurs for £1700.

The club eventually decided to appoint a new manager and approached Lloyd-Davies, an in house move anticipating the legendary boot-room! Davies declined the offer claiming business and family loyalties in Wales. Davies owned a tobacconist's shop in the small town of Cefn in North Wales, his family stayed there whilst Davies lodged in Northampton. Instead the directors turned to another senior professional on the staff and appointed Fred Lessons.

It appears that Lessons had complete faith in Walter who began the first game of the season. This ended in a 1-1 draw against Crystal Palace. The Echo reported, “Good as was the Palace half-line, I do not think it did more effective work than Tull, Manning and Tomkins. The play of both sets of halves was the feature of a keenly fought game.” Walter was to hold his place throughout the season but for a brief spell injured in December. In all Tull played in 34 of the 38 league fixtures and appeared for the first time, in the Cobblers' colours, in the F.A. Cup.

This tie like the previous season pitched the Cobblers against league opposition, on this occasion in the form of Derby County. Derby, founder members of the league, were in the first division, although that season were destined to finish bottom and were relegated with another founder member Preston North End. In a strange twist of fate both clubs were to finish first and second the following season - they would take their places back in the first division only after the Great War. The two teams were accompanied by Arsenal as the F.A. authorized an expansion of both divisions. This caused a stir as the Gunners had only finished fifth in the table. Barnsley who were third complained to no avail and were forced to wait another 78 years for promotion to the elite. Arsenal's chairman Henry Norris was considered to have persuaded the authorities of Arsenal's "potential" as he had invested heavily in the club. Then as now money was a powerful argument.

For the record Derby edged past the Cobblers 1-0. Strangely both sides viewed the game with something less than enthusiasm. Derby struggling in the league feared defeat in the first round at the hands of an "inferior" team. The Cobblers, as ever, were looking for a bigger draw and a larger share of the gate.

Walter returned for the game after straining a muscle in the Southampton match on December 13th. The "Daily Echo" on the day of the tie recorded in its report the respective heights and weights of the two teams. Walter was listed as 5ft 8 ins tall and weighing 12st 6lbs. Only one player on either side measured 6ft, Lawrence the Derby goalkeeper. I'm not sure how many current Premiership or Nationwide sides would dare take the field with such a Lilliputian defence. No wonder contemporary educational reform was concerned with the provision of school meals and the revision of physical education.

As noted, the game was tight and conditions underfoot certainly did not help matters, the "Daily Echo", perhaps Tapper, reported that, "...the ball played all sorts of tricks in the mud..." Walter got some important early touches but he must have found the ground difficult having just returned from injury, it seemed to have an adverse effect according to the report in the later stages of the game. Nevertheless Derby took the lead after twenty minutes and managed to hold on to it, failing narrowly in the closing minutes to make the scoreline more comfortable, "…and another attack on the Northampton goal followed. Barnes hit the post and Leonard sent over. Thorpe was given a warm time, and shots were sent in at him from all angles."

Whilst Derby were much relieved to hold on other league teams were not so lucky. Swindon, Southern League Champions that season, were victorious over Manchester United by the same 1-0 scoreline; as were Gillingham, 13th in the Southern League, over Blackpool. Elsewhere Queens Park Rangers and Brighton were "flying the flag" for the southerners with a 3-2 victory and 1-1 draw against Bristol City and Oldham respectively. Brighton holding an Oldham side destined to finish in third place in the First Division that year.

Other results included Huddersfield's 3-0 win over London Caledonians, Glossop's 2-1 win over Everton and Sunderland's 9-0 victory over Chatham.

Walter's old club Spurs played out a thrilling 5-5 draw, away to Leicester Fosse. City doesn't have the same kind of ring… how about it Leicester?

One footnote to the Derby game concerned Davies' commitment to the Cobblers as he played in the cup tie in preference to playing for Wales on the same day in Belfast, a game which Ireland won 1-0. This obviously did his international chances no harm as he played against Scotland in Wrexham and England in Bristol. The first game ended 0-0 and the second was close but ultimately led to a 4-3 victory for England. The following season he appeared in all the Home internationals, the 1914 season ended with Wales achieving identical results: a draw with Scotland and two defeats!

The following week the Cobblers played away to Queen's Park Rangers, at Park Royal. The game ended 0-0, with the home side having the best chances. Walter's contribution was mainly defensive and the reports of the match only mention him conceding corners to the impressive Birch; the purple prose of those contemporary reports never fail to impress: "Thorpe fisted out in great style," "Rangers went off at a great dash", "a great sigh of relief went up". Although an adjoining report gives it a run for its money, the story concerned a traffic fatality: "The evidence for the Crown in the sequel to the motor-car fatality near Stamford in which Ronald C. Maxwell, student, 44 Cathcart Road, London was charged that he, on the 13th December, 1913 at Thornhaugh did feloniously kill and slay one, Arthur Mason, by running into him with a motor-car, was concluded before the Peterborough Justices on Thursday, and Sir Ryland Atkins formally asked the Bench to commit the accused for trial at the Assizes." A sentence that would have taxed "Tapper's" eloquence!

Tull was now a regular and the side had a very settled look once again as seven other players played even more games than Walter, with goalkeeper Thorpe appearing in one less. Lessons himself played 35 games mainly at centre half. It was the solidity of the half back line consisting as if did of the player manager, Tull and Manning that received most of the plaudits as the team rose from the previous season's tenth place finish to third place. The free scoring days of Herbert Chapman's sides seemed to be behind them as the final tally for of fifty goals attests. The defence conceded only thirty-seven, at marginally under one a game, surprisingly Reading and Crystal Palace conceded even fewer. Nevertheless this was an impressive effort by Walter and his defensive colleagues.

Walter clearly earmarked for defensive duties did not score during the season, in fact all of his goals for Northampton came in his first abbreviated season for the club. A remark in The Echo's report of the Cobblers v Merthyr game summed up Walter's season in front of the opponents' goal, "Tull attempting to shoot aimed badly." One other feature worth noting about the season was the number of drawn games, nineteen in all or exactly 50% of all league matches. If four more goals had been scored at the right times the championship would have gone to the County Ground...if as already noted, a big word!

The drawn games were commented on by "Old Crock" (any relation to "Tapper"?) in the "Wellingborough News". OC's flowing language a match for Tapper anyday:

"It is getting somewhat fatiguing to the many supporters of the Cobblers to repeatedly hear of their pets' inability to put the required finishing touches to their splendid efforts. Again on Saturday they failed to steer clear of that formidable (to Northampton) "draw vice". It is true that "half a loaf is better than no bread" but when one contemplates the record the Cobblers would have possessed with the addition of a single goal in so many matches, it makes one's mouth water. The 18th draw came on Good Friday, when the Cobblers share six goals with Watford. Their 19th on Saturday was creditable, as their antagonists were last season's shield winners Plymouth Argyle, the result being 2-2."

Although overall it was a successful season, luck clearly did not run with the Cobblers during October: they lost to Fulham in the annual Hospital Cup game. This was an annual invitation game to raise funds for Northampton General Hospital. Over ten thousand people turned up for the match and there was great dissatisfaction as a Fulham reserve team took to the field; the first team playing in a London Charity cup fixture. The crowd's feelings were not improved as the Londoners reserve side won by 2-1. Sadly a far more poignant event was about to take place. On the eighteenth of October just before a home game against Millwall, Lloyd-Davies was informed that his young son had died. Bravely Davies played in the game before returning home for the funeral. A week later Walter recorded that the away game at Exeter was delayed because of problems travelling to the game, leaving Northampton Castle Station at 8.45 the team did not reach St.

James' Park until minutes before the kick off and as a result lost 0-2. Strangely he was involved in a similar situation a month later when Southampton appeared at the County Ground. The referee made the teams change straight round at the interval claiming fading light.

Davies may have received some scrap of comfort at the end of the season when the club granted him a benefit game. He chose as opposition a Welsh Select XI which included, amongst others, the legendary Billy Meredith. Meredith's career spanned thirty years and included spells at both Manchester United and Manchester City. He claimed to have played in over 1500 matches, these included 48 games for Wales, his last cap gained at the ripe old age of 45. Whenever and wherever he played he was rarely seen without a toothpick in his mouth, a dangerous accompaniment in the days when full-backs introduced themselves by dumping their opponents into the second or third row of the stand.

Toothpick or not, Meredith will be remembered as one of the founder members of the Player's Union [14] and when the F.A. ordered all players to resign from this organisation, Meredith refused as did many of his Manchester United colleagues. The F.A. no doubt feared a revolution in wage demands, insurance against injury and heaven forbid freedom of contract. The situation was accelerating towards a strike by all players, thus in September 1909 (Walter must have been wondering about his fledgling career) the F.A. backed down and the union was allowed, albeit in an emasculated form. One particular bone of contention for the F.A. was the players wearing, during games, an armband with the Player's Union logo and title, this was banned by the authorities in 1910.

There had been a mixed reaction from the players and clubs to the proposed strike, Colm Kerrigan notes that George Hilsdon, the English international forward and his Chelsea team-mates, all union members, were less than enthusiastic

14 John Bell of Everton had tried but failed to form a player's union a few years before.

about the prospect. Many chairmen were less than pleased although retaining some sympathy for the players. H.G. Norris, one time Fulham chairman was against the wage cap but said, "…the professional player has been called a 'white slave', yet a salary of £4 per week, with three months idleness, is the sort of life that many thousands …would jump at."

Meredith never slow to criticise injustice blamed the players: "I confess that the bulk of the players have not shown much pluck in the matter…". Had the players shown the "pluck" we may never have heard of Jimmy Hill.Charlie Roberts, Meredith's captain at Manchester United shared Meredith's distain of many of the players saying they had turned their backs on the only power they had.

Meredith as mentioned played well into his forties and was a member of the Welsh side which defeated England at Highbury in 1920, this victory clinched the Home Championship for the Welsh for only the second time. Meredith's swansong came in 1924, incredibly in his fiftieth year he turned out in the FA Cup semi-final for Manchester City against Newcastle - unfortunately for Meredith the impossible dream proved just that as Newcastle edged City by one goal to nil. In his retirement Meredith like many ex-pros took to pub management and even managed to play a role in the film "The Ball of Fortune", about soccer bribery. He died on the 19th April 1958, just two months after the Munich tragedy.

Although Lloyd-Davies' Cobblers' side lost this encounter 0-5, a healthy crowd of five thousand turned out to show their appreciation. I am certain Davies appreciated the effort and I am also certain Walter would have enjoyed playing in such august company. Whilst on the subject of Meredith it is hard not to draw comparison with Walter. Both men saw soccer as more of a weekend activity rather than a profession, it was almost as if there was something to be disapproved of, the long hours when others were working and players were idle. Meredith like Walter had given up a good job, in the mining industry, to turn professional and like Walter he had battled with his conscience before the financial lure of soccer became inescapable. For a few years Meredith had tried to do both before Manchester City insisted he quit his job at Black Park Colliery. Both men came from strong Methodist backgrounds, sharing a sense of loyalty with the friends and peers, sharing a strong sense of duty - look no further than Meredith's stand on behalf of the Player's Union or Walter's speedy volunteering for the army. Both loved soccer! Where they differed was quite clearly in Meredith's ability to court controversy. He had been cited in a bribery scandal following Manchester City's final game in 1906 against Aston Villa, City needed to win to stand any chance of winning the league. It was alleged Meredith offered Alec Leake, the Villa captain, £10 to throw the game. In the even Villa won 3-2 and Newcastle who had to lose to give City a sniff of the title won as well. The Player's Union fiasco led to a lengthy ban from the game. He even managed to alienate the Manchester United directors after his testimonial game, to such an extent the full amount raised was not paid in its entirety for eight years. In his private life Meredith fared little better facing a bankruptcy suit when his sports goods business was burnt to the ground.

It is perhaps worth noting that of the sixteen caps Lloyd Davies won, Meredith played in fifteen of those games. Of those fifteen games Wales won 4, drew 5 and lost 7.

At least at the end of the season Walter could consider himself an integral part of the team, he must have been very happy with the way things were developing and looking forward to the new season. He might perhaps have been looking forward to a new season in Scotland as it had widely been reported that Glasgow Rangers were interested in signing Walter. Their interest was certainly sparked by Walter's brother Edward, who by now a successful dentist in Glasgow and playing local amateur football, got to know several people at Rangers, most notably Jimmy Bowie who in his time played for the club, became its chairman as well as that of the Scottish Football Association. Edward got to know him when they both played for Girvan Athletic. It must have been very tempting for Walter to move, to go and live with his brother and indeed by then many of the family had moved north too. By the time of Walter's death in 1918 it seems only William and Miriam were not living with the Warnocks at this second home in Girvan in Ayrshire.

A move to Rangers must have been very tempting professionally for Walter. Then as now, Rangers and Celtic were the two big clubs in Scotland. Between the 1900 and 1915-16 seasons, they won the title no fewer than 14 times. In the same period Celtic took the Scottish Cup 6 times to Rangers once! Rangers were also runners-up on two further occasions.

One unusual footnote to a war time Rangers game, which has nothing whatsoever to do with the subject of this book was: due to wartime transport the side began a game against Falkirk with only 9 men. A feature the 2000-01 team will know all about! Having finished one European tie with 9 men a few weeks later in December 2000 they repeated the feat away to Hearts.

The fact remains Rangers were a very big club and Walter must have been very flattered to have received such interest.

Chapter Eight

Events in Sarajevo shaped the 1914-15 season, although there were few people who believed that the war would last long. “Over before Christmas” was the popular refrain. Few also believed the war would involve anymore than the regular armies of the combatants. These thoughts alongside a desire to maintain both soldiers' and the public's morale encouraged the authorities to continue the league fixtures until the end of the normal season.

Obviously there was a lot of misgiving about continuing with the league programme in 1914-15 and one voice which was very loud and very quick to denounce this was F.N. Charrington part of the famous brewing dynasty. He was a committed socialist (with a small 's') and philanthropist; he campaigned vigorously for soccer to be stopped. He saw the anathema of playing sport whilst others were going to the front. Charrington was no lone voice and his sentiments echoed those of the famous writer Rudyard Kipling expressed at the height of the Boer War. Charrington also claimed the support of Admiral Jellicoe, commander of the Grand Fleet. Jellicoe's reply to this was non-committal. Punch magazine joined the debate on the 21st October 1914- a cartoon featuring Mr.Punch facing a serious looking player holding a ball in a striped kit was saying,

“No doubt you can make money in this field, my friend, but there's only one field where you can get honour.”

In parenthesis were the words, “The council of the F.A. apparently proposes to carry out the full programme of the Cup Competition, just as if the country did not need the services of all its athletes for the serious business of war.”

Another powerful voice joined the debate about the continuation of professional sport, W.G. Grace. Grace the greatest sportsman of his generation, now aged sixty-six, wrote in “The Sportsman,” “I think the time has arrived when the county cricket season should be closed, for it is not fitting

Northampton Town F.C.
Walter, third right middle.
Eric Tompkins extreme right middle.

at a time like this that able-bodied men should be playing cricket by day and pleasure seekers look on. I should like to see all first class cricketers of suitable age set a good example and come to the help of their country without delay in its hour of need."

Nevertheless the football season began. The opening games saw few changes in the Northampton line up regulars like: Clipston, Freeman, Hughes, Lloyd-Davies, Manning, Thorpe, Tomkins and Tull were ready for another tilt at the Southern League title. In Walter's case thoughts of joining Rangers may have been put on hold due to the international crisis, almost certainly he had decided to "join up" as soon as possible. It has been suggested that he reached an agreement to join the Glasgow club when hostilities ceased. If this was so it was a promise which tragically could not be honoured.

The hopes of maintaining any sense of normality were soon dispelled when many of the early games were attended by recruiting officers looking for volunteers. Similar recruiting drives took place in virtually every football ground in the country from Old Trafford to the County Ground. In London Clapton Orient's ground was a particularly fertile recruiting area for Hackney residents, West Ham's for the people of Ilford and East Ham. Recruitment was haphazard, for example, on the 20th November Goodison Park saw Everton record a handsome 7-1 win over Sunderland; scores of men came forward before, during and after the match. On the same day at St. Andrew's, Birmingham, it was claimed no-one enlisted. As the weeks ran up to Christmas several of the Cobblers' home matches actually showed significantly increased attendances due, at least in part, to a large Territorial Army base being set up in the town. The site in Clare Street still exists, although other barracks in the town and adjoining Wootton have long since been turned into housing estates and flats.

During matches collections were taken and used to send essentials to the troops at the front. Soccer was not the only sport in the town doing its bit for the war effort; a rugby international was played at Franklins Gardens (home of the renowned Northampton RUFC, commonly referred to as the 'Saints' due to the area in which the ground was situated, St James's End). The game took place on the 30th January 1915, again the simple motives to help raise money and encourage men to enlist. Edgar Mobbs, Northampton and England rugby player and serving army officer helped to organise the game and exhorted the crowd afterwards to join the cause. Sadly Mobbs was killed in 1917, his memorial the annual East Midland XV versus the Barbarians or more simply Mobbs' match.

During the first half of the season Walter played twenty-two consecutive matches for the first team, his longest unbroken sequence. As ever he proved his versatility turning out, for the first four games, at left-half, moving to centre-forward for an away game against Millwall, then playing at right-half where he stayed for the majority of the thirty-three league and cup games he played that season.

A novelty for the side and for Walter occurred on January 9th, when the side travelled to Grimsby, then in the second division. The Cobblers came back with a very creditable 3-0 win. It is not recorded if the team were given the traditional box of fish, which the home directors gave to visiting sides. Certainly skate, cod, depths, trawling, netting and other associations would have been manna from heaven for Tapper et al.

This was Northampton's first victory in the cup for three years and Walter's first and last such experience. The second round did not send the Cobblers to heaven but somewhere much more mundane; Hull City, another second division team. This resulted in a 2-1 defeat, no box of fish but some very positive reports in the local press especially as Hull were to finish seventh in their division.

Hopes of achieving a better position than the previous season's third place had been hampered by a slow start, one win in the opening five games: a one-nil victory over Southend. To be fair to the Cobblers, the first six games featured five away matches. Nevertheless results improved and from January 23rd to March 27th, the side was unbeaten recording five wins and four draws. Thus the side was still in contention vying with Watford, West Ham and Reading for the top places. Unfortunately three of the last four games ended in defeat, these included consecutive 5-2 losses to Southampton and Cardiff. The Cobblers last season before football ceased left them in fifth place, with Watford as champions.

By the end of the season gates were noticeably affected. A comparison with the previous season shows that season's highest gate was 9,000 for games against Coventry and Norwich over the Christmas period the average stood at around 6,000. The following year the best attended fixtures were against Reading 8,500 and for the final game against Millwall 8,000. The season's average was nearer 4,000 with crowds of only 1500 and 1000 for West Ham and Portsmouth respectively.

The final game of the season and as noted the final game until 1919/20 season was at home to Millwall. The side and Walter signed off in style, the nightmare 5-2 defeats were forgotten as the Cobblers recorded a 5-0 victory.

Walter who had actually missed the previous two games, some confirmation of his value, returned for this final match. The "Echo", recorded his return noting, "...Whittaker who now like Tull and Whitworth had donned Khaki." Everyone by now was realising the folly of the idea of the war being over by Christmas and these three were just a small example of the hundreds of sportsmen who had enlisted.

Over 7,000, many in uniform, saw an exciting contest which at least for a long period in the second half was not as one sided as the score might suggest. For the record the teams were:

Northampton - Thorpe, Clipston, Davies, Tull, Manning, Tomkins, Hughes, Smith, Whitworth, Lockett and Freeman.

Millwall - Wood, Fort, Woodley, Nuttall, Wilson, Nicholl, Whittaker, Williams, Davis, Moody and Lamb.

The scorers were Hughes and Whitworth who scored two apiece and Lockett.Walter's contribution alongside fellow half-back Tomkins was summarised by the "Echo's" reporter: "The Northampton halves were playing splendidly." Who could have known this would be Walter's and many others throughout the Leagues, last professional game? I am sure that with all Walter's innate modesty this anonymous praise would have pleased him greatly.

Another little 'footnote' to the game was also highlighted by the reporter to do with Welsh troops in the town: "Of special interest to the Welsh troops in the town was that there was a Welsh international on each side, viz., Davis (centre forward for Millwall) and Lloyd-Davies."

It seems ironic that in the next column to the match report the paper carried a story about the opening of the new eighteen hole golf course on the Kettering Road, where a series of mixed foursomes were played. For some at least life continued as normal.

I wonder if the players, soccer and golf, had considered the fate of one of England's recent soccer heroes, Steve Bloomer - Derby County? Poor old Bloomer retired in 1914 and took a coaching job abroad. Yes, you guessed it, in Germany! At the outbreak of war he and other fellow footballers were interned and they spent a relatively comfortable time in the Ruhleben camp, amongst other things playing football on the nearby racecourse. Certainly luckier in the long run than many of his fellow professionals including Walter who fought and suffered on the Western Front.

Chapter Nine

It was announced during April 1915 that there would be no organised soccer the following season because of the war. As news of the escalating casualties spread, public opinion hardened against this entertainment whilst men were dying and being maimed for their country.

The curtain was brought down on soccer in England by the Khaki Cup Final of 1915, so called because of the number of soldiers in uniform among the crowd. Sheffield United triumphed over Chelsea by three goals to nil. One Chelsea player owed his place to the magnanimous gesture of Vivien Woodward (more of whom later) who back on leave from the Army, refused to take his deputy's place in the team. Presenting the cup after the game, Lord Derby encouraged the teams to go forward and play "for England now".

Thus at the end of the 1914-15 season league football was formally abandoned. Ironically had Walter joined Rangers he would have found a completely different picture because league games continued almost unhindered in Scotland although not without criticism. The Glasgow Herald asked, "What does it matter about Rangers and Celtic when the greatest of all internationals is being played on the continent?" There was some concession to the war over cup-ties. It was not until 1917-18 that Dundee, Aberdeen and Raith Rovers were asked to withdraw from the league on the basis that the statutory five and a half day working week made it impossible for the West of Scotland clubs to arrive on time for a 3 o'clock kick off. However in England some football was continued and Northampton following the example of many other clubs allowed a band of amateurs and guests to represent them at the County Ground. Games were regionalised and were played ostensibly to raise money for the war effort and to entertain the troops who were waiting to go to, or return to the front [15]. Quite a few of the players were the very men awaiting orders. Several of the Cobblers' recent players made appearances including: Lloyd-Davies, as well as Fanny Walden and Jock Manning.

There were some amazing results from this period, the games were obviously all friendlies against local teams or against Army elevens who were in the area. Many of these teams had ex-professionals in their sides, so some of the games were of a decent standard. Two particularly interesting results came over a Christmas period. On Christmas Day the 'team' travelled to Luton and lost 2-9; four days later, they entertained Luton with a makeshift side that included goalkeeper Newman at wing-half, but they won 8-2! War-time football did not lend itself to settled squads or to tight defences or perhaps tight defences was the key, over-imbibing the Xmas spirit!

In the Home Counties, a competition called the London Combination was set up involving both Football and Southern League sides. Games were to be played on Saturdays and public holidays, players received no payments and all proceeds went to the war effort. Players did not often receive medals or cups as metal was needed in the armaments industry.

Women's teams were also organized throughout the country to raise money for the wounded and bereaved families. Pioneers of women's soccer, Lady Florence Dixie and Nettie Honeyball who perhaps saw soccer as a symbol of the greater struggle for equality and the vote now channelled their energies into raising money. Perhaps the most famous team were the Dick, Kerr Company Ladies' team from Preston. The team raised a great deal of money during and after the war for numerous charities. At their peak, during 1920, they played before 53,000 at Goodison Park beating St Helen's Ladies by four goals to nil. One of the quirkier charity

15 Scottish clubs like their English counterparts were doing the best for the war effort, for example during May 1916 the Champions Celtic played the rest of the League, Celtic were narrowly beaten 1-0. Celtic like many other English and Scots clubs provided a disabled enclosure for the war wounded.

Posters asking for volunteers

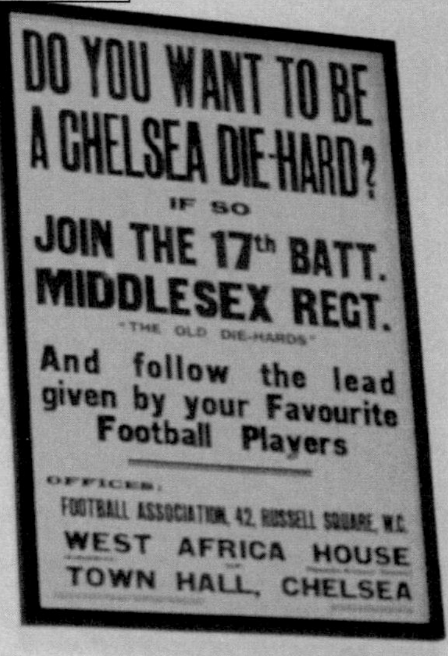

games was played at Southern League Reading's Elm Park ground, The Armless Men versus the Ladies' XI. The men were convalescing Canadian troops, their opponents a group of local English women. For the record the girls won 8-5 and the troops were armless only because their hands were tied behind their backs. Which raises the question, what did they do about a throw in? The F.A's thanks for such sterling efforts was a 1921 ban and any member club of the F.A. who allowed women's games faced the same expulsion. The ban remained in force until 1970.

Walter did not feature in any of the Cobbler's games not that he had turned his back on football. In fact during training and before embarkation to France he had guested for Fulham in the aforementioned London Combination. Ironically Walter played a last game at White Hart Lane when Fulham lost 3-1 to Spurs. A year later the ground was commandeered by the Ministry of Munitions and turned into a gas mask factory.

As previously noted in the Millwall match report Walter had joined up, in fact he had been the first Northampton player to do so, being joined quite quickly by team mate George Whitworth. Walter had joined the 17th Battalion of the Middlesex Regiment also known as the 1st Football. One recruiting poster used the following message: "Do you want to be a Chelsea Diehard? Join the 17th Battalion Middlesex Regiment… and follow the lead given by your favourite football players!" [16] Walter was thus following a pattern developed at the time to join up alongside friends, workmates, neighbours and family. Many units were organised to allow men to serve together on the basis of a sport or a region - even small neighbourhoods. The appeal to the recruiters was obvious such groupings were good for morale and encouraged whole sections of the community to come forward rather than in dribs and drabs. These many "Pals" regiments were also particularly associated with close knit communities like the northern mill towns, towns like Accrington, Burnley and Colne.

16 For the record more players joined from Clapton Orient than any other side.

The reverse side to that particular coin was soon to be tragically observed when whole communities were shorn of their young men at one terrible stroke. The 'Pals' battalions were a peculiarly English response to the war- not favoured in Scotland which favoured a less homogenous approach.

By November 1914, the press claimed that 100,000 men had joined up as a result of the recruiting drives connected with soccer. It was also claimed that of 5,000 professional footballers, nearly 50% had also joined the colours. Later research placed the number of players volunteering in hundreds rather than thousands. Overall an incredible 2,500,000 men had answered the call to volunteer by the end of 1915.

The 1st Football was not only example of soccer doing its bit for King and country, in Scotland, for example, the Hearts players joined up together, alongside many of their supporters. There is a monument to their bravery outside Haymarket station in Edinburgh.

It would be hard to imagine such a mass rush of volunteering today from any professional squad, the eclectic mix inhabiting the majority of dressing rooms would probably guarantee internment! The Chelsea team circa 2000 would with one or two exceptions be the other side of the Maginot Line. It is however a humbling experience to witness such confidence and loyalty. Walter was only one of many professionals who quickly joined the colours. The 1st Football were commanded by Major Frank Buckley, ex-footballer and a man who would build a fearsome reputation as a manager of Wolverhampton Wanderers.

Other well known volunteers included Vivien Woodward, as mentioned previously, it was his move from Spurs to Chelsea that prompted Tottenham to sign Walter. Woodward played numerous times for the England Amateur XI and also represented the full England side on twenty three occasions, scoring a staggering 28 goals. This fact alone shows how highly Spurs must have rated Tull as a replacement for a man with that kind of record. Amongst Woodward's other honours

Walter Tull in uniform, picture taken shortly after his commission as Second Lieutenant, Middlesex Regiment

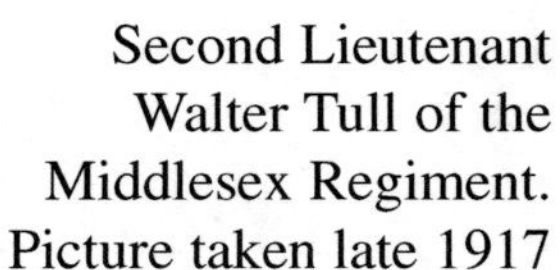

Second Lieutenant Walter Tull of the Middlesex Regiment. Picture taken late 1917

were his captaining the United Kingdom's Olympic side which won the gold medals at the 1908 and 1912 tournaments. As well as being a gifted footballer Woodward was a keen cricketer and by profession an architect, in many ways he embodied the Edwardian all-rounder, something in the style of C.B. Fry. To add to his impressive C.V. he became director of Chelsea F.C. and even tried his hand at farming. He survived the war and died aged 74, in 1954.

In so many ways Woodward was everything that Walter was not: the gentleman, the officer, the amateur. Walter did not have the background for such luxuries he was working class, a private soldier and a professional - it was a chasm but one Walter would bridge. It is highly unlikely that the pair met one another at this time, as Woodward was wounded within a few days at the front.

Not all players were as keen to join up, Colm Kerrigan in his biography of George Hilsdon ("Gatling Gun George Hilsdon - London's First Football Star") records George's absence from the West Ham team, the very month conscription was introduced. A story was handed down that George was caught in a chicken run whilst trying to evade recruiting officers! Ironically George was to see action, as did Walter, during Ludendorff's Spring Offensive in 1918. Another strange twist was that Walter would have certainly met George when West Ham visited the County Ground in March 1915 - the 1-1 draw particularly due to Hilsdon's missed penalty.

Walter had been finally posted to France in November 1915, one can only imagine the mixture of emotions he must have felt: excitement, fear, the almost certain knowledge that he would be wounded or worse. He had read about the second battle of Ypres, where the Germans used gas for the first time, a battle lasting over a month to gain three miles.

The staggering British losses at Aubers Ridge and Festubert or the battle of Loos - no pun required. It is rather ironic to many footballers in a similar situation at the start of the second world war many of whom were selected to serve as physical training instructors, no insult is intended or any slur implied rather the Army saw the better deployment of their expertise. Even then many "instructors" saw service in Europe and Africa. It is difficult to believe that Walter would have followed any other path than the one he did.

Nevertheless the next six months saw the usual routine of weeks in the trenches and weeks resting behind the lines; the classic mixture of boredom and terror. He was no doubt looking forward to leave and seeing family and friends again. Walter's brother William had also joined up, he was a "Sapper" with the Royal Engineers, both brothers kept up a regular correspondence between themselves and with family and friends at home. Walter wrote to Mr. Hodgson-Smith, another member of staff at Bonner Road, about the boredom and monotony of life behind the front trenches: "It is a very monotonous life out here when one is supposed to be resting, and most of the boys prefer the excitement of the trenches to the comparative inaction whilst in reserve.

I have only run across one Old Boy since I've been out here. A lad named Hudson who is in the 1st K.R.R's and had just come back from leave-called in on me one day and we had a nice chat together".

The powerful influence of Bonner Road on Walter and the loyalty it engendered is clear from each letter he wrote home, in one way it was his family, he had after all been directly connected with it for over a decade. In the same letter he expressed concern for Mrs Jeffrey, a former cook at the Home, he was worried that she was struggling, 'to make ends meet' .[17]

The monotony was partially cured by soccer, there were many games organised to help keep spirits up and to alleviate

17 NCH Archive

the crushing boredom. Then, as now, soccer presented an opportunity for the men to mix, to forget for a while the circumstances surrounding them. The most famous example of this came on Christmas Day, 1914, when both British and German troops laid down their weapons and celebrated the unofficial truce with an impromptu game of soccer. There are many accounts of this including - Frank Richards' memoirs “Old Soldiers Never Die”.

Many makeshift teams were chosen to create an added “spice” to these games, one fixture played over Christmas 1915, featured the men of Kettering and Wellingborough versus those of Rushden and Clipstone. This was a game Walter qualified for, unfortunately for him it was played between the ranks of the Northamptonshire Yeomanry. For the record the game ended 1-1. An indication of the morale boosting effect is given by a certain Corporal Cleaver's remarks: “We are about four miles from the firing line, but expect to have a scrap with them any time now, and we will let them know the Kettering boys are there” (“Wellingborough News” 8/1/15).

Many myths have been created about the galvanising effect the game had upon the troops, reaching its apotheosis in the East Surrey's attack on the Montauban Ridge on the Somme. Captain Nevill is reported to have encouraged his men to attack the German trenches by producing several footballs to kick about as they advanced.Allegedly Nevill had messages printed on the footballs; one bearing the note, “The Great European Cup Tie Final East Surreys v Bavarians.” Another carried, “No Referee” which was a way of telling the men not to treat the Germans too gently. True or not, Nevill was killed, the ridge was captured and many medals were awarded. The “Daily Mail” recorded the heroics in verse:

“On through the hail of slaughter
Where gallant comrades fall,
Where blood is poured like water,
They drive the trickling ball…”

Whilst the British press recorded events in such elevated style, the German press used it as propaganda to show the absurdity of British command. Nevertheless General Jack, in July the following year was claiming, no British troops ever travel without footballs or the energy to kick them.Some of the impromptu games had a purpose beyond raising morale. The Royal Engineers organized regular gas mask games whereby when the whistle went for kick-off each player had to take out his mask and fit it properly. No player could touch the ball until the mask was secured. During the games the referee would stop proceedings and order the removal of the masks. This time the masks had to be put away before the players could resume their game. The aim was to familiarize the "sappers" with the dexterity needed to use the masks. Almost certainly William would have been involved in such an exercise. Just for good measure the games were played in full uniform.

By May 1916 Walter was sent home suffering either from Trench fever or "shell shock" or under its modern definition Post Traumatic Stress Syndrome. Both conditions affected thousands of troops throughout the war. Walter was fortunate to be treated appropriately. Many others were not as fortunate, many driven to desert their posts and indeed hundreds were executed for such a crime. There were many sympathetic and diligent doctors who worked tirelessly with these exhausted, distressed and often broken men their efforts rewarded by returning their charges to the fighting, to conditions as bad or worse than they had left. The doctors and psychologists, men like W.H.R. Rivers, celebrated in Pat Barker's, "The Ghost Road" must have questioned the validity of their work. Ironically one of the military hospitals that Walter could have attended was in Sandgate, Folkestone, although there is no existing record of this, one can only hope, that was the case.

Walter was considered fit enough to return to duty in September, once again he was fortunate he had missed his battalion's involvement in the beginning of the infamous Battle of the Somme. The 17th Middlesex had been involved in heavy fighting around Delville Wood and were part of an attack on the village of Guillemont; the attempts to clear Delville of the Germans was particularly vicious and random with close hand to hand fighting. One officer quaintly and modestly understated the task as "odious". It is well chronicled: the suffering, the slaughter, the mind-blowing casualties, the great losses sustained by both sides. The absolute carnage of that terrible battle is still celebrated in film, for example William Boyd's work "The Trench" which acknowledges the bloodiest day of slaughter in the history of the British Army. Who watching the film could forget the final frozen image of Billy McFarlane falling backwards and spewing his brains across the screen.

Walter survived his latest stint in the line and was allowed further leave over the Christmas period. Visiting Scotland he spent time with Edward and his fiancée Elizabeth. Edward met Elizabeth or Betty in Aberdeen. Her father A.B.Hutchison was the senior Baillie of the city. Walter no doubt looked forward to the future wedding when he would appear as the best man. Before this could happen there was another duty to fulfil as Walter was to join an officer training course.

The course was certainly not unusual for a vaguely promising N.C.O. (Walter had been promoted to sergeant), the casualties suffered by junior officers dictated as much. What was positively staggering and virtually unknown, as far as the British Army was concerned, was the complete absence of black infantry officers. Technically Walter's commission was impossible for under military law "Negroes" could not give orders to white soldiers. [18]

18 Today we still view the Great War as a European one, it is easy to overlook the contributions of the "Empire", the Indians, Africans, West Indians, et al. India for example sent 140,000 men to the Western Front, 90,000 infantrymen and 50,000 in labour companies of these nearly 60,000 were killed or wounded. Even these professional soldiers were not deemed worthy of commanding themselves, white officers were given charge, this again puts Walter's achievement into perspective.

Clearly, whatever the casualties, Walter could not have reached the point without the support and recommendation of white serving officers - once more this speaks volumes for the efficiency, courage and popularity of the man. Almost certainly his prowess as a footballer contributed to his chances of promotion. Almost certainly his experience of racial abuse would have armed him against any pettiness or jealousy his commission might bring.

It must be noted that in the early days of the war the officer class was drawn exclusively from the public and sometimes grammar schools; boys who had gone through the traditional training in the schools' O.T.C.'s. How many of the Old Etonians lost in the war, some 1,100 plus, were not officers? How many of the 707 ex-Wellington boys? Sue Smart in her book "When Heroes Die" records the loss of many old Greshamians. Gresham, one of the newer public schools, under the stewardship of George Howson was a small school with just 287 on roll, 101 old boys were lost by the end of the war. Howson like many schoolmasters encouraged his pupils to do their duty and whilst applauding those who joined the ranks urged later volunteers to put their OTC training to proper use and serve as officers. Against this background of loss the brighter and more diligent NCO's were encouraged to fill the alarming gaps that were always evident late in the war. Enter second lieutenant Tull!

Walter was sent to Gailles in Scotland to undergo officer training. This was quite a stroke of luck for him, Gailles was a picturesque small town on the Ayrshire coast surrounded by golf courses. It gave Walter a vital break from the war and it also placed him near to his brother Edward. During the weeks of training the two brothers and their sister Cissie met frequently. Walter stayed at the Warnocks' home and no doubt much conversation was given to the future and plans for when the war ended. Edward still had hopes of Walter moving to Scotland and playing for Rangers. Already it seems that Walter was considering a future outside football. It was

Edward's dream to get all the family to Scotland. Walter was however thinking over a military alternative by joining the Royal West Indian regiment. This news would have been devastating to Edward.

Sadly whilst Walter was training in Scotland, his battalion was involved in further heavy fighting around Waterlot Farm on the Somme. They sustained unsupportable losses, to such an extent that the survivors were disbanded and sent to other units. Meanwhile the newly commissioned Walter Tull was sent back to join the 23rd Middlesex Battalion. He joined the Battalion near to Ypres and quickly wrote home describing his new situation. Shortly after this he was involved in the Battle of Messines.

Earlier in the war a certain corporal served at Messines on the German side of the lines: Mr Schickelgruber himself - the man with the funny moustache - Adolf Hitler! Apparently he spent quite a lot of time painting local scenes, whilst there was anything left to paint presumably! Writing to his landlord back in Munich he recorded this impression of the area: "For the past two months our regiment has been constantly in the front line between Messines and Wyteschaete. The meadows and fields look like bottomless swamps, while the roads are covered ankle deep in mud… The air has been trembling under the screams and the roar of grenades and the bursting of shells. What is most dreadful is when the guns begin to spit across the whole front at night… but nothing is ever going to shift us from here." Ironic last words, I am sure he probably said something similar twenty odd years later about Stalingrad.

The battle of Messines or rather the battle for the Messines ridge which overlooked the British lines in the Ypres salient, had long been considered by the British generals as a priority.[19] It gave the German forces a clear advantage in observing the

19 To such an extent that a huge scale model was built at Scherpenberg, it was designed by the sculptor Cecil Thomas, a serving officer in the 23rd Middlesex Regiment. The vast majority of Allied Officers involved in the assault visited the reconstruction to familiarise themselves with the ground they were about to attack.

allied movements. Thus during the early months of 1917, the British tunnelling companies started to drive shafts towards the crest. Nineteen galleries were created culminating in mine chambers packed with tons of high explosive. (The dangers of tunnelling are brilliantly described in "Birdsong" by Sebastian Faulks)

Just before dawn on the 7th June, 1917, the mines were detonated, with a noise so huge it was heard in London. The blast itself was detected on the observatory seismograph on the Isle of Wight. Nine divisions of infantry moved towards the German lines, many of them like Walter, veterans of the early days of the Somme.

Prior to the huge explosion, three weeks of bombardment had 'softened' the German defences. When the assault waves arrived on the crest, they found such defenders as survived unable to offer resistance. The British suffered negligible casualties. Philip Gibbs, a war correspondent who witnessed the scene, described the shattered remnants of the German trenches as: "The most diabolical splendour I have seen."

By now technology was rapidly catching up with the needs of war. During the bombardment the British employed their new Thermit bombs. Fired from mortars, Thermit a caustic mixture of powdered aluminium and iron oxide which when ignited caused a startling chemical reaction which generated thousands of degrees of raw heat. The horror multiplied by the air bursts scattering molten metal on the enemy. Trenches and dug outs burst into flame and were still smouldering hours later.

Following the seizure of the ridge Walter and the 23rd Middlesex had the job of clearing the area around the Comines Canal. The task was quite straightforward at first, moving along the canal in a diamond formation they picked up many prisoners coming under only sporadic fire. Near Houthem heavier pressure was brought to bear and eventually forced them to pull back. A German Spotter plane began to direct fire on them and as the commanding officer commented things, "looked exceedingly bad". Eventually the British artillery found its range and the Middlesex moved forward again. By the end of the operation many prisoners were taken as well as four pieces of field artillery. Once again Walter was involved in a dangerous, complex situation and emerged unscathed and reputation unstained. Overall the battle was a great success the Allies captured 7,000 Germans, they seized 48 big guns, over 200 heavy machine guns and killed at least 13,000 of the enemy.

Within days of clearing the canal, the 23rd Middlesex were moved to the south of Ypres and in a letter to Eddie Walter described his first duty in their latest position :

"I joined the Battalion on Saturday when they came back from the line and was at once posted to "D" coy. On Monday at noon my C.O. detailed me to go up and inspect the portion of trench we were to hold as we were to go up that night. Three other Subs. and myself started off about 1.30 but Fritzy was shelling the back area like a demon… We were lucky and got to a tunnel which would help us on our way considerably. Unfortunately the outlet was flooded and we got soaked up to our hips." On successfully reaching the line Walter and his colleagues spoke to the Adjutant of the battalion to be relieved and following a break for tea made their way to the forward positions. The entire journey of no more than three miles took five hours. By 1.00 a.m. the following morning his company was in position. At this point Walter was told he was not needed and, "I wasn't long in getting a move on." The journey back was equally time consuming and at one point, having picked his way back through the tunnel, he begged a "seat" with a platoon of signallers. Spending several hours with them he discovered one of his new found friends had been at school with Northampton team mate Jock Manning. Reinforced with a tot of rum, Walter continued his journey and feeling weak recalled he had had nothing to eat for over seventeen hours. Reinforced by tea and sausages at a YMCA canteen he finally reached camp for a ,"good tub and got into bed." He later recorded a night's rest which, "All the guns in France couldn't wake me". Accompanying the letter was a mark note which he euphemistically recorded as, "You can guess where it came from." As a P.S. he added, "Am applying for a transfer to the West Indian Regiment when the Battalion comes out tomorrow."

The application was put on hold as six weeks later another part of Haig's plan for the Western front came to fruition - the third battle of Ypres or more commonly known as Passchendaele. On the 16th July a 10 day artillery bombardment began followed by an infantry advance on a front stretching fifteen miles.

Unfortunately just as on the Somme, the battle was a futile and tragic exercise perhaps over confident after the success at Messines, the British High Command overestimated the effects of the artillery and underestimated the difficulties caused by the terrain. Heavy rains had turned the battlefield into a swamp. We are used to the grainy photos of men trudging through the shell cratered, muddy countryside. Of horses desperately pulling on the artillery limbes, so much it has almost become a cliché. How physically debilitating it must have been, how ingrained in each man's psyche. Walter mentioned in his letters the mud and the problems caused by it even when resting behind the lines he noted the area was, "... very bleak and desolate with a super abundance of mud on the roads." How much worse on the battlefield!

When the village of Passchendaele was finally captured in November it was at a cost of over 500,000 casualties. The only memorable feature of the whole fiasco was the grit and courage of the men who fought. Men like Walter Tull! Men who had gone through hell - the hell of, "bodies split, heads blown off, grovelling fear, shrieking fear, unspeakable fear! The world made mud!" (J.L. Carr "A Month in the Country." Penguin).

In terms of ground won, the Allies could calculate five miles or approximately 100,000 casualties per mile. Their epitaph can be left to John McCrae's poem, written during the second battle of Ypres, "In Flanders Field":

We are the Dead. Short days ago
We lived felt dawn, saw sunset glow,
Loved, and were loved, and now we lie
In Flanders fields."

McCrae died almost two months to the day before Walter, in January 1918, as a result of complications following a bout of pneumonia. He had seen service in the Boer War and at the time of his death was a colonel in the medical corps.

Chapter Ten

Shortly after the Battle of Ypres Walter and the 23rd Battalion were posted to Italy; Italy had entered the war late in May 1915, claiming Italian speaking areas occupied by former ally Austria. Italy was especially keen to get the Adriatic port of Trieste. Two years of war with small gains and mounting losses seriously undermined the Italians' resolve and when the Austrians attacked the Italian army at its weakest point Caporetto, it looked as if the whole front would collapse. The Italians sustained 40,000 casualties, many more were taken prisoner and many more deserted. Thus five British Divisions and six French Divisions were sent to bolster the Italian line which had reformed on the River Piave just north of Venice. Reinforced and with the knowledge that the Italians were now fighting for their homeland they resisted with a vigour previously unnoticed!

At one point during the Battle of Piave, Walter was mentioned in despatches for leading his men with "coolness and bravery".The occasion for this was a night raid on enemy positions, Walter was charged with leading a covering party across the Piave. The successful raid completed, he brought his men back safely. Major General Sydney Lawford the commander of the 41st division placed on record : "…my appreciation of your gallantry and coolness. You were one of the first to cross the river prior to the raid on the 1st/ 2nd January, 1918 and during the raid you took the covering party of the main body across and brought them back without a casualty in spite of heavy fire." There have been suggestions that had a white officer performed his duties so well a more tangible recognition would have been his, a military cross for example! Gradually the situation hardened into the familiar entrenched stalemate witnessed on the Western Front. In some ways serving in Italy must have provided, initially at least, something of a contrast and a relief from the mud and slaughter of Messines and Passchendale.

An indication of the difference is given in the first chapter of Ernest Hemingway's novel “A Farewell To Arms” he describes part of the Piave region, the rich plains the orchards and brown mountains. There was fighting in the mountains and at night and the odd flash from the artillery. Certainly the nights were cool but nothing like as miserable as Flanders.

Mountains, plains, orchards, it was indeed a far cry from the faceless and featureless land of the Western Front. Orchard trees rather than incinerated stumps - it was still deadly but must have appeared a heavenly vision compared to the hellish terrain of the Somme. There were still all the familiar routines and mundane dangers and as romantic as Hemingway's prose becomes even he admits to, perhaps, the biggest enemy of all - the weather,the rain and with it came a different problem cholera. Eventually it was checked and in the end only seven thousand died of it in the army. Only seven thousand!

The novel was based upon Hemmingway's own experiences and unlike Walter he served as a non-combatant, initially driving ambulances. Hoping to see more action he volunteered to move to the Piave front and it was here that he was wounded in July 1918, he eerily described the experience later as,seeing his spirit come from his body and fly around. Despite this alarming experience he was moved to a military hospital in Milan where he gradually recovered. Later he was awarded the Italian Silver Cross of War and was lauded as a hero by the American press. On this occasion Walter was lucky, certainly luckier than Hemmingway he survived the Italian campaign unscathed, reputation enhanced. His reward, return to the Western Front. No Silver Cross, no Military Cross- were the military authorities operating a colour bar?

Family Group

Walter in uniform with brother Edward, sister Cecilia ("Cissie") and Edward's adoptive mother Mrs Warnock ("mater")

The picture is dated 1917 and was probably taken at the Warnock family home in Scotland

Chapter Eleven

As mentioned Walter led his men with great coolness and efficiency whilst stationed on the Piave Front. Shortly after the January raid in which Walter "won his spurs" he was granted leave, which he spent in Rushden.

The question of leave was uppermost in every soldier's mind, thoughts of home and family, release from the boredom and the danger, making plans for the future. Walter came home following his bout of shell shock, after his officer training and just after his service in Italy. As limited as this was others were often less fortunate as a sad letter to the "Rushden Echo" shows:

"Dear Sir,

Why should the best part of the men in a company get home on leave and not the others? In the case I have in mind they have stopped two months now and yet others have been coming all the time and only been out there six to nine months instead of twelve months or more. It is very disheartening."

This sad missive was simply signed a soldier's wife.

How much harder might it have been for the husbands and fathers? Walter had a close family of brothers and sisters and even on the evidence of his limited leave allocation he was probably amongst the luckier soldiers at the front.

Nevertheless whilst on that final leave Walter heard the news that he and his regiment were being posted back to France.

By now Walter was a veteran of several campaigns he had earned the 1914-15 Star, served on two major fronts, seen countless battles and witnessed as much slaughter and mayhem as any other serving soldier. He had suffered, recovered, endured and still served the country selflessly and did so without complaint.

Walter returned to France to face his and possibly the British Army's greatest test. In early 1918 the prospects of an end to the war were no nearer. Morale was low, divisions on the front were seriously undermanned. Lloyd-George, the British Prime Minister was holding men back in Britain fearing no doubt that Haig would sacrifice them in more disastrous and futile gestures masquerading as 'decisive' offensives. Production was down in almost every sphere. Almost every family was grieving over the loss of a loved one. Food shortages, rationing and queues were common sights. Many workers were becoming restless with conditions, talk of a different form of government was rife. In Germany the situation was, if anything, worse. A naval blockade was successfully hampering all kinds of imports. Grain production was half its pre-war level. German politicians were quick to realise the impact America would soon have on the war. Many politicians were ready to accept a peace settlement but the military faction held sway and they were contemplating a last, desperate effort. In some minds at least the possibility of a German victory still existed.

The German general Erich Ludendorff assumed that by freeing himself and the army of the trench mentality, his men would be able to break through the British lines on the Somme. Thus early in 1918 large numbers of troops were transferred from the East where Russia, following the revolution, was no longer fighting. The Kaiserschlacht (Kaiser's Battle) began on the 21st March with a short but very heavy, artillery bombardment. The German artillery opened fire at 4.40 am firing the first of some 3 million rounds they fired that day. Unsurprisingly there was little response from the allied artillery, one officer Lieutenant Scott of the Somerset Light Infantry noted there was no answering fire from..“our guns, I sent a runner back with a message to this effect but I got no reply . It was the first time I had been in an attack and I was surprised at how few men were being killed although many were wounded. We sent these down to the dug outs. There wasn't much I could do as an officer except walk up and down." A Private in the Machine Gun Battalion was more succinct, "It seemed like the bowels of the earth had erupted." In fact all anyone could do at this point was to sit tight, try to protect themselves as much as they could, keep their weapons handy and prepare for whatever next the Germans had in mind.

They did not have to wait long as the German's elite storm-troops led the way, they were lightly armed and moved very quickly, bypassing strong points they made crucial breaks in the weakest parts of the British defences. Aided by a heavy fog they caused pandemonium in the British lines. British artillery was rendered useless it could not react to the swiftness and suddenness of the enemy's advance and with the Germans now sweeping behind the front allied artillery action could not guarantee not killing their own. In the first few hours confusion and panic gripped the British - success seemed assured for the Germans.

A runner for the 7th Royal West Kent regiment brought a message to headquarters, from a Colonel near Ly Fontaine. The colonel claimed to be holding out although surrounded and with visibility down to just forty yards.

Amidst the madness many British units were issued the order to stand and fight to the last round and the last man - the situation was desperate. Other units were cut off, men lost contact with their officers. One private in the Sherwood Forresters noted that he and a friend had been asleep when the rest of his company moved out. An alert officer noting the absence came back for them, he spoke of the confusion, the erratic shelling and of fire fights with small numbers of marauding enemy soldiers. One local French peasant caught in the mayhem stood waving at the passing English shouting, "Anglais soldats no bon!"

In a few days the German Army had advanced over forty miles on a broad front. It had achieved what no other force had done in all the years of trench warfare. This advance

Walter's name recorded along with other 2nd Lieutenants

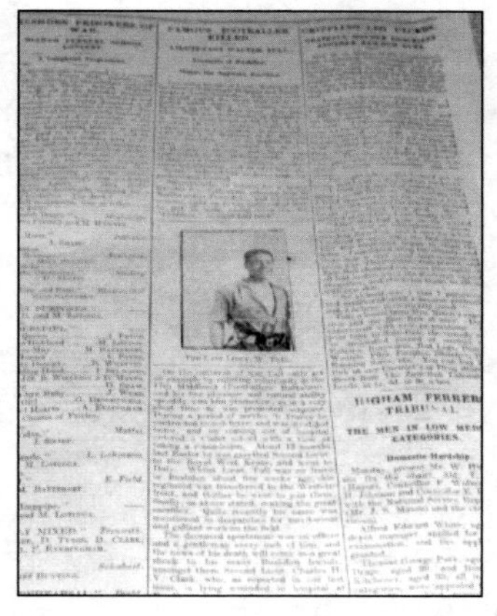

HIGHAM FERRERS TRIBUNAL

Report of Walter's death - Rushden Echo

made a complete mockery of any of the previous Allied (or indeed German) efforts when the capture of a few hundred yards or a couple of trenches was considered a victory equivalent to Waterloo!

However the grim reality was still the huge number of losses on both sides it has been estimated that on the first day of the battle over 18,000 died, nearly 39,000 wounded and over 21,000 taken prisoner. In this final category the figures make for very interesting reading, the British captured a mere 300 men compared to nearly 21,000 British soldiers captured.

The "Northampton Echo's" report of events was officially upbeat, admitting that: "The German offensive launched yesterday morning covered nearly the whole of the British front south from the Scarpe to the Oise, a distance of over 50 miles. It is on a larger scale than any during the war.

Sir Douglas Haig telegraphed last night that the vast attack had been pressed with the greatest vigour throughout the day, and that last night severe fighting continued on the whole front."

The results of the first day's fighting are summarised by the "Times" as follows: The enemy broke through our outpost positions and succeeded in penetrating out battle positions in certain parts of the front. The attacks were delivered in large masses, and caused the Germans exceptionally heavy losses. Captured maps show that on no part of the long front of attack had the enemy obtained his objectives." Hindsight is a great quality and perhaps no-one at that point had a clear view of events but no mention of British casualties, the Germans huge advance dismissed, major German casualties noted - sounds like propaganda!

As for Walter's role in these events his battalion had been sent up to the line east of Bapaume, on the 21st March. The following day they marched to Achiet-le-Petit where dinners were served and ammunition handed out to the companies. By mid afternoon lorries carried the battalion to the Bapaume-Arras road where they bivouaced in a field until midnight. A shell hit the encampment killing eight and wounding twelve.

Shortly after midnight the 23rd marched up to support trenches at Beugny and were spread over a series of hastily dug trenches. By 10.30 a.m. on the 23rd the lines were subjected to a "tornado of shells", the subsequent enemy advance drove the Middlesex back to west of Beugny. In the evening the 23rd were relieved and moved back to the aerodrome at Favreuil, casualties for the day included four dead, thirty nine wounded and twelve missing. Even here they continued to engage the enemy.

The enemy's advance remained unchecked; the 23rd battalion fell further back to the reserve line and as others fell back the troops were reorganized; assisted by Royal Engineers the Battalion dug in until dawn, according to the Battalion Diary casualties amounted to 104 killed, wounded or missing, although no details of the fighting were given.

Early the following morning the Germans opened with heavy shell fire. Shortly after 8 a.m. their infantry attacked. The 23rd fell back across the Arras-Bapaume road where bitter fighting ensued, although forced back the battalion retired in good order. From the next line behind Bihucourt along a railway embankment counter attacks were ordered. Walter was ordered to clear an enemy machine gun post which was dominating the village main road. Reports soon came back that Walter had received a head wound leading his men towards the village. According to witnesses he died almost immediately, attempts were made to bring his body back to the British line; unfortunately the concentrated enemy fire caused the soldiers to abandon his body and save themselves. One of the soldiers who put his own life at risk trying to carry Walter was Private T. Billingham who pre-war had played in goal for Leicester Fosse.

The losses suffered on the 25th were heavy, as well as Walter,Lieutenant Colonel Haig-Brown and Lieutenant Pitty were also killed. Captain Hammond, Lieutenants Green and Barton wounded. Thirteen others were killed and 99 wounded or posted as missing.

The news of Walter's death was given initially to Edward who was the nominated next of kin he described it simply as, "the worst moment of my life". Sadly his body was never recovered and there was nothing to record his death except his name on a memorial wall at the Fauborg - Amiens war cemetery [22]. His commanding officer who broke the awful news to Edward remarked in tones completely unlike the usual dispassionate and "anonymous" telegram that Walter was, "..popular throughout the battalion. He was brave and conscientious… The battalion and company have lost a faithful officer and personally I have lost a friend."

The obituaries that followed echoed these sentiments it is worth recording the "Rushden Echo's" eulogy in full:

It appeared in the paper on the 12th April 1918, under the heading "Famous Footballer Killed. Lieutenant Walter Tull. Formerly of Rushden makes the supreme sacrifice". The many friends of Lieutenant Walter Tull the former Tottenham Hotspur and Northampton Town footballer, will hear with profound regret the news that he is reported killed during the recent heavy fighting on the Western Front. The late Lieutenant Tull was well known in Rushden as, being a close friend of 1st A.M.E.F. Tomkins (RFC), another county footballer he made his residence in the country with Miss A.S. Williams of 39 Queen Street, Rushden. Left an orphan at an early age, he was brought up at Dr Stephenson's Homes, and later was apprenticed to the printing trade. His abilities as a footballer, however, speedily attracted attention, and an offer from the "Spurs" induced him to leave trade for professional football.

Subsequently, in return for a heavy transfer fee, Tottenham released him to Northampton Town Football Club and for several seasons right up to the outbreak of war he put in some useful work for the "Cobblers" as right half back.

22 The cemetery contains the graves of 2,647 British soldiers most of whom died from their wounds. The memorial walls commemorate 35,928 whose bodies were never recovered. There is also a smaller memorial in honour of British Airmen

On the outbreak of war Tull early set an example by enlisting voluntarily in the 17th Middlesex (footballers Battalion) and his fine physique and natural ability won him promotion, as in a very short time he was promoted sergeant. During a period of service in France he contracted trench fever, and was invalided home, and on coming out of hospital entered a cadet school with a view of taking a commission. About twelve months last Easter he was gazetted second lieutenant to the Roy West Kents (sic) and went to Italy. Whilst Lieutenant Tull was on leave in Rushden about five weeks ago his regiment was transferred to the Western Front, and thither he went to join them finally, as above stated, making the great sacrifice. Quite recently his name was mentioned in despatches for meritorious and gallant work on the field.

The deceased sportsman was an officer and a gentleman every inch of him and the news of his death will come as a great shock to his many Rushden friends, amongst them Second Lieutenant H.V.Clark, who, as reported in our last issue is lying wounded in hospital at Reading. On more than one occasion the late Lieutenant Tull played for Rushden Town Cricket Club."

It is ironic to note that on the day of Walter's death his local paper reported that after very fierce fighting on the Somme there was little cause for alarm. The War Office was quoted as saying the troops although tired were in good heart and that the enemy progressed at the cost of heavy sacrifice to themselves.

In the same newspaper reports of other losses were recorded. Needless to say Walter was no exception during that furious assault by the German Army. One report highlighted the fears for another Second Lieutenant, Henry Bandey, formerly an employee at the CWS Boot Works in Rushden. The article noted he had been missing since the 21st March. The pathos of the request for information, from his father a local hotel proprieter of Woodford Halse, brings a lump to the throat even now. One cannot help but wonder what was the better alternative, a confirmed death as in Walter's case or the faint, flicker of hope of a miracle; sadly for both families there was no miracle.

Meanwhile it was Edward's sad duty to inform the home of Walter's death. He wrote simply and movingly in a brief letter dated the 8th April, 1918.

"Dear Sir,

You will be sorry to learn of the death of my brother W.D.J. Tull. He was killed in action on the 25th March. He was a Second Lieutenant in the Middlesex Regiment and being a Homeboy, as I am myself, I thought it right to write to you.

Yours sincerely

Edward Tull-Warnock" [23]

The reply no less dignified emphasised that Walter was, "a fine speciman of manhood and as you know was a great favourite whilst he was in the home". [24]

23 NCH Archive
24 NCH Archive

Chapter Twelve

It is difficult at this distance to appreciate what a pioneer Walter Tull was. It takes a very special person to surmount the barriers of class and colour and to establish themselves at the highest level. Today it is still difficult for a black person to overcome the barrier of racism, how much harder it was in Edwardian Britain.

We take for granted the number of black footballers and perhaps many younger supporters assume this was always so. Walter was the first black outfield player. Arthur Wharton is credited with being the first black player in England, appearing in goal for the famous Preston North End side of the late 1980's. Wharton a gifted athlete did not make the mark upon the game that Walter sustained over a number of years.

Much has been made of the difficulties facing black players over the last few years and rightly so, everyone of them has had to battle for the recognition that their white counterparts could take for granted. It was not until the 1970's that black became "groovy" with the appearance of the "Three Degrees", West Bromich Albion's Cyrille Regis, Laurie Cunningham and Brendan Batson. Even then they faced much abuse, one small consolation was they, at least, had each other for support. Walter faced such abuse alone with courage and dignity. It seems so obvious that when Len Cantello was granted a testimonial game, for his sterling service to West Brom that he could call upon a fixture against a Black XI led by his colleague Cyrille Regis. Walter was the solitary black player in the football/southern leagues prior to the First World War!

It has already been noted how special it is to make a mark in one's profession when battling the twin evils of class and colour prejudice. Football, at least playing wise, offered fewer barriers than the military. In the army Walter raised himself to a pinnacle unheard of for a black man.

Walter's courage, charisma and sheer fortitude allowed him to reach a position which was technically impossible in the British Army. The "Manual of Military Law" (1914) declared that, "any Negro or person of colour" could not be an army officer. His bravery, popularity and a terrifying casualty list defied such nonsense. How much of an example must this have been to the hundreds of thousands of non-white troops serving in the British forces at the time and since? Black men who fought side by side with their white contemporaries. Men who died alongside their white contemporaries. Men who when the war was over were repatriated without the slightest acknowledgement of their role in the war. What must it have meant to the West Indian, Indian, Ghurkha and other units to see this tiny chink in the establishment's blinkered and racist policy?

The pragmatism of the British Government's deployment of Black troops and ancillaries can be best judged by their stance at the 1919 Conference, when Japan proposed a clause in the League of Nations Covenant providing for religious equality of races. The Japanese, our allies during the war, expected that for reasons of international diplomacy this request would be "rubber stamped". To their horror Australia, Britain and the USA took strong exception to the suggestion. The Australian Prime Minister called the amendment "dangerous nonsense". Lord Cecil, Britain's delegate saw it as a challenge to the management of the Empire. Harold Nicolson, another member of the British delegation went further saying he dreaded a situation where there was implied equality of yellow and white men and worse still anything that might imply the equality of white and black. What a sordid rebuff to Walter and the thousands and upon thousands of "non-whites" who lost their lives! [25]

Students of literature and history will know of the role of Wilfred Owen and his moving accounts of life on the Western Front immortalised in such poems as, "Dulce Et Decorum Est", "Anthem For A Doomed Youth". He too died late in the war, he too died having battled to a lesser degree against the class consciousness of the establishment. How close their experiences, how close their ends. How different their recognition and celebration. Yet Walter's example and courage deserve to be published and acknowledged equally. His voice, unprinted, shows the same critique of the brutality and hopelessness of war and more importantly the brutality and futility of racism.

Walter's "legacy" to the army is certainly not as impressive as soccer. The bare facts reveal that things have not changed much since Walter's time. There are approximately 150 black or Asian officers in the army today, the most senior two colonels in the medical corps. The Millennium intake at Sandhurst featured only 23 blacks or Asians amongst its 910 entry, at the same time there were no ethnic minority instructors. For an institution which has supposedly re-invented itself as a champion of equality these figures do not look too positive.

The campaign for Racial Equality challenged the army as to why Great Britain has not got an equivalent to Colin Powell in the USA. The reason offered was that personnel could not be recruited like senior managers in industry and had to be trained from their recruitment. Therefore the first black general was still many years away!

Channel 4's programme "The New Model Army" highlighted some alarming opinions. Professor Christopher Mulland (Focus Management Consultancy) claimed that there is still a white officer class commanding a black underclass. The officer commanding the Ethnic Minority Recruiting Team suggested that "They're frightened of discipline" quite

25 A similar loss of faith in Britain occurred in India. British Rule was enshrined in the Defence Act of India which was scheduled to run to 1919- there was a reasonable hope, given their sacrifices during the war, that some degree of independence would be granted to the country. As with the Japanese, the Indians were to be disappointed, not only was there no encouragement but subsequent legislation came down hard on the pro-independence lobby.

who the "they" are and allowing for editing leaves this comment ambiguous.

The programme followed the training of a young, black officer and even then the onus was placed very firmly on his public school background, his Christian beliefs et al. The final message for promotion was simply to be the right officer in the right regiment at the right time. There's no doubt that Walter met those criteria and as a result paid the ultimate price.

One danger for the unwary is that Walter might be considered a novelty, a freak rather than the pioneer and inspiration he deserves to be recognised as. We have noted contemporary match programmes referred to him as "Darkie". It would be equally unjust to think he was some kind of token - he was not and gradually his worth is being belatedly recognised. The late Bernie Grant M.P. recorded simply that Walter: "…to have done what he did, he must have been a remarkable man." A fine tribute from another remarkable man.

More concrete tributes, literally so, have been accorded to Walter, a memorial stone was erected at the southern end of Sixfields stadium in Northampton. The monument, the central point, in a small garden of remembrance, was officially unveiled in July 1999 and immediately received the plaudits of Prime Minister Tony Blair. He described Walter as, "a beacon of courage whose life is an inspiration. To his fans at Northampton Town F.C., he was a star wing half who turned out for the first team over 100 times. To his fellow soldiers in the Great War, he was a hero and friend, a natural leader who rose from the ranks to become an officer and died leading an attack in the Battle of the Somme. He was the first black officer in the British Army and one of the first black professional footballers in this country."

Another "monument" to his example is to be found in the Football Against Racism movement and the increasing number of clubs who have adopted an official policy against racism.

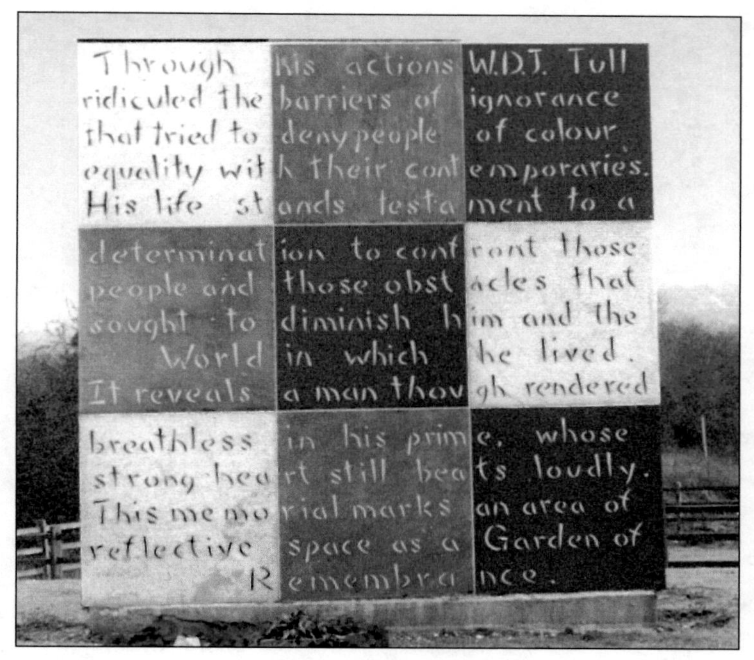

Sixfields Memorial

Northampton Town F.C. has played a leading role in this area and amongst other things seek to: "…take action against any supporter who engages in racist abuse, racist chanting or intimidation, whether inside or outside the stadium." Thus more than eighty years after his death, having entered a new Millennium we will remember him when we say kick racism out of football and out of our society.

Today in theory at least, no black player should have to suffer the indignities Walter did at Bristol City. With local authorities working in concert with the clubs and with the backing of the government's Football Task Force much is being done to "outlaw" racism for good. Fans groups via fanzines and other means are helping to change perceptions, many clubs have produced their own anti racist literature,

Sixfields Memorial Plaque

pressure has been brought to bear on right wing groups, which were commonly seen in and around grounds during the 1990's. Much credit for this must go to a great fan of Walter's, Sir Herman Ousley (Chairman of the Campaign for Racial Equality), his skill and determination to engage the football authorities in this process has been crucial, UEFA has thrown its weight behind the campaign announcing, in February 2001, measures which would be taken against clubs in their competitions which did not control racist behaviour in and around their stadia.

Another tribute to Walter, ironic since he has lain for so long in an unmarked grave, came in the summer of 2000, when a road leading to Sixfields Stadium was renamed Walter Tull Way. The ceremony was performed by Northampton South M.P. Tony Clarke, himself a Northampton Town F.C. director. Mr Clarke remarked that, “Walter Tull acts as a focus for the garden of remembrance. There are already three people's ashes there - local people, mainly football fans, who wanted their ashes within the stadium. It's become a place of reflection. It's heartening to see.”

Shortly after the Probation Service opened an office to deal with young offenders; the large building, formerly an insurance office, stands at the bottom of Bridge Street in Northampton town centre. The building named in honour of Walter has written into its deeds that the name will stay in perpetuity regardless of the use of the building.

Heartening indeed that such a remarkable man is now getting the attention and praise he so richly deserved. Let us leave the final words to the words on the reverse of the memorial stone at Sixfields Stadium which provide an eloquent and moving eulogy: -

Through his actions W.D.J. Tull ridiculed the barriers of ignorance that tried to deny people of colour equality with their contemporaries. His life stands testament to a determination to confront those people and those obstacles that sought to diminish him and the world in which he lived. It reveals a man though rendered breathless in his prime whose strong heart still beats loudly.

The words are Phil Vasili's.

Walter Tull House - Northampton

Chapter Thirteen

A final world must be included about the contrast of opportunity for a black footballer like Walter and the situation now. In the years since the First World War many black players managed to forge careers with professional clubs: men such as Alfred Charles at Southampton, Jack Leslie (Plymouth), Roy Brown (Stoke), Gil Heon (Glasgow Celtic), Lindy Delapherla (Portsmouth), Albert Johansson (Leeds), Clyde Best (West Ham), Mike Thebicock will always be remembered at Everton for his two goals in the FA Cup Final against Sheffield Wednesday.

It has been noted already that the 1970's saw a real breakthrough in terms of selection of black players, the final big hurdle was made when Viv Anderson became the first to win a full England Cap in November 1978. Four years on 13 black players were selected for both the senior and U.21 sides. By June 1984 John Barnes scored his famous goal against Brazil at the Maracana Stadium.

Elsewhere the barriers were coming down Scotland had selected Paul Wilson for a game against Spain in the mid seventies (it is now suggested Scotland's first black player was capped in the 1880's), the Republic of Ireland capped Paul McGrath, in 1985, versus Italy when he appeared as a substitute. Wales were well ahead of this having given Eddie Paris of Bradford his first and only cap in 1932 against Northern Ireland. England could also claim that their first non-white capped player was Hong Y "Frank" Soo who played nine times during the war, these games were later declared unofficial. A further breakthrough occurred when Paul Ince took over the England captaincy for a few games in the 1990's.

By the end of the 1980's nearly every team in the football league would be fielding one or two black players. Statistics, dangerous at the best of times, show that there has been an approximately 200% increase in the number of black players in the Football League between 1986-1998. Looking at current premiership squads, approximately 15% of players are black.

The profile of Black players has been raised in other ways such as the transfer system. Managers are happy to pay millions for Black players without concern of the lazy stereotype. The current record transfer between English clubs is held by Rio Ferdinand. Stan Collymore has moved several times for large fees, Liverpool paying Forest £8.5 million. Les Ferdinand not to be outdone by Rio moved to Newcastle for £6 million, Andy Cole from Newcastle to Manchester United for £7 million.

The intriguing question is quite simply how does today's Black footballers' experience differ to that of Walter Tull? One might reasonably assume that over the last eighty years things have indeed changed and progress made, that the bigots who abused Walter are no more. It is however clear that such progress is not a linear process in which rights increase with time, we might assume Frank Soo or in later years Albert Johansson faced less problems. If this were so we would expect John Barnes' dream goal against Brazil to be celebrated by all England fans. However on the return journey from Rio, a group of "supposed" fans claimed the goal did not count because John was Black!

The treatment meted out to the West Brom stars of the seventies has already been noted and reinforced by other players; fans, of course, failing significantly to note that their own team had Black players but at least these were "their own".

Mark Walters' move to Rangers (Mark became the first Black player some seventy years after Walter Tull's aborted move) proved difficult. The Rangers' fans still called him "Sootie" or "Jaffa" (black on the outside, orange within!). Those same fans claimed at least signing a Black was not as bad as signing a Catholic, although manager Graeme Souness did that too.

At least we might reasonably assume the troubles faced by players are the product of rival fans' antipathy and are not from any other source. There was never a suggestion that Walter Tull had anything but very positive relationships with his clubs, managers and peers. If only life were so simple, Tony Ford who holds the Football League Appearance Record for an outfield player notes that things within some clubs were not always positive although the situation is improving, managers no longer pick “niggers” v. whites five-a-side games. The racial abuse on field has all but disappeared, in spite of some high profile recent clashes between Ian Wright and Peter Schmeichal and Stan Collymore and Steve Harkness over alleged racial taunts. At all levels this kind of behaviour is being treated with the utmost severity and rightly so. One Marine AFC player, accused of the same, never played for the side again having been sent off for comments made to a young Black opponent.

Managers are not yet totally immune to intolerant outbursts as the example by the then Wales manager Bobby Gould against Nathan Blake shows. Gould was forced to climb down and make a public apology. In the ever more complex world of modern football there are other potentially dangerous areas as seen in the debacle, during April, 2001, between one of Brentford's sponsors and one of their Black players Gavin Mahon. Mahon voted the February player of the month claims he was denied his prize - the use of a luxury car - because of his colour. The claim supported by the club's commercial manager and rejected by the sponsors was investigated by Jaguar Cars.

Recent developments would seem to suggest the possibility of progress and enlightenment co-existing alongside extreme prejudice. There is much to applaud in the Anti Racist initiatives and the adoption of Anti Racist policies by such clubs as Northampton Town, Sheffield Utd and Bradford City but there is still some work to be done.

One such area concerns the problems facing any young

black players hoping to make their way in professional football the 'class/race' barrier still exists. Phil Vasili argues that the decrease in schools' football disproportionately affects youngsters from disadvantaged backgrounds. Instead of playing at school where, "if you are good enough you play" the emphasis is now much upon junior teams. In these teams the social and economic background of the family has a great significance upon whether the youngster has access to sport. The difficulties of those players from disadvantaged families, one parent or deprived backgrounds to be able to buy kit, get transport to and from training, pay subs, present huge problems. Vasili also notes that a greater proportion of African-Caribbean children live in the deprived, inner city areas than their white peers; the same reasons apply to the access to Football Academies and Centres of Excellence. There are of course exceptions to the rule Hedley King (Spurs) and Ashley Cole (Arsenal) have acknowledged the debt owed to the sacrifices made by their mothers in encouraging their ambitions.

Many black players are still taking the same route into the professional game as Walter by playing non-league and then signing for a league team at a later date. Ian Wright is perhaps the prime example but Stan Collymore and Les Ferdinand both signed at the age of 20 for Crystal Palace and QPR respectively. Northampton's Chris Freestone first signed professional forms aged 23. Steve Brown also signed for the Cobblers aged 20 after a successful stint with local side Vanaid who won the National Sunday League Cup. It was Brown who committed the cardinal sin of removing his shirt during Wycombe's FA cup quarter final win over Leicester City and received the red card for his efforts. Fortunately he was able to play in the tense 2-1 defeat against Liverpool in the semi-final.

If Walter's example of courage and forebearance is to be realised it will require some investment in the grass roots of the game. Efforts must be made to allow the game to be accessed by all parts of the community rich and poor, black and white. Schools will need to revise this provision - alas poor teachers already burdened in so many ways, so wake up Government! Football academies and centres of excellence will perhaps need to look back critically at their recruitment criteria. Phil Vasili expresses the problem eloquently, to eradicate the inequalities necessitating the democratic control of power and as soccer is a plutocracy with the handful of monied people ruling the roost the chances of this sharing of power are slim at present.

It would be nice to assume that the nonsense of Scientific Racism had disappeared by the end of the twentieth century but also it would appear to be alive and well in Spain. In a speech made in 1996 the leader of the Basque right wing group PNV suggested that true Basques were distinguishable because of the extra bone to be found at the back of their skulls - the "Spanish" were merely a mongrel race snoozing away in the Andalusian sun. ("Morbo, The Story of Spanish Football" by Phil Ball (WSC).

Sixfields Memorial

Chapter Fourteen

What happened to some of the other main personalities in Walter's story? Walter's brother Eddie or Edward James Alexander was the fourth child of Daniel and Alice Palmer. He was born in 1886, two years before Walter. When their father died because both were too young to contribute to the family budget and as we know they were sent to the Bonner Road Children's Home.

Edward was fortunate to be adopted by Mr and Mrs Warnock of Glasgow and was educated at Allan Glen's School in the city. He then attended Glasgow University where he gained the degree of L.D.S. in 1910. It was probably around this time that he changed his surname to Tull-Warnock to acknowledge the help his adopted parents had given him.

Having qualified as a dentist he practised in Aberdeen for two years before returning to Glasgow to establish his own business, this proved so successful that within another two years he was able to open a branch practice in nearby Girvan.

Whilst in Aberdeen Edward met his future wife Elizabeth Hutchison, they were married in 1918. The wedding was deliberately kept 'low key' in view of Walter's recent death. In 1920 Elizabeth gave birth to a daughter Jean who remained their only child.

Like Walter, Edward was a keen and gifted sportsman. It has already been mentioned that he played soccer at a high level in the amateur game representing Ayr Parkhouse and Ballantrae amongst others. His obituary featured in the local Girvan paper noted, "…he was a grand little sportsman, a tricky inside forward and a menace in the goal area."

He was also noted as an accomplished golfer becoming a member of the famous Turnberry Golf Club. Given the haughty and exclusive nature of such an institution it says much for Edward's popularity that he obtained a membership. Whilst there he won several trophies including the Weir Trophy and the Glasgow Dental Cup which was held for three

successive seasons, 1928-30.
Among other sports he counted bowls where he was regarded as a "...strong opponent and enjoyed nothing better than a fighting finish."
Amongst Edward's other interests was music, he had a fine baritone voice and as well as singing in his local Methodist Church, he was particularly fond of "Negro Spiritual" music. He was a timeless supporter of good causes and in 1936, received the compliment of being elected President of the Allan Glen's Old Boys' Club.
Sadly Edward fell ill just after his 64th birthday and he died on the 3rd December, 1950. The affection in which he was held in the area is best summed up by the last few lines of his obituary. "To one who knew him intimately it can be said he truly loved his Girvan and his many friends in the town. He has passed on, leaving in our hearts a lasting and fragrant memory."
A remarkable man it would seem, just like his brother!
Sometime teammate Fanny Walden was born in the same year as Walter 1888, in the Northamptonshire town of Wellingborough. 'Fanny' as he became known was actually christened Frederick Ingram. The nickname derived from a lady who kept a corner shop near his home. Standing just 5 feet 2 inches tall he became a pacey and exceptionally skilful wing forward as well as accomplished county cricketer; his soccer career began at Wellingbourh Redwell and at the age of 18 he signed for the Cobblers.

Starring for Northampton he caught the eye of several clubs not least that of Leeds City with Herbert Chapman then in charge. As previously mentioned the move to Leeds was thwarted but was quickly followed by his transfer to Tottenham, where he became an international. His international career spanned eight years, even so he won just two caps the first in 1914 v Scotland the second in 1922 v Wales. The former game ended 1-3 to Scotland, the latter played at Liverpool's Anfield ground was won by England 1-0. Walden still holds one record he is the shortest forward ever to appear for England. His lack of inches and youthful appearance prompted one gateman to eject him from the ground with the words "Go away sonny" when he arrived late to an away fixture during the 19/12/13 season. In stature he resembled Terry Dyson, winger in the great Spurs "Double" side of 1960/61. Like Dyson he was excellent with either foot and never shirked from the physical side of the game. Fanny enjoyed a very successful time at Spurs, his only regret, apart from losing years to the war, was missing the 1921 F.A. Cup Final against Wolves due to injury.

Even at Spurs he was not entirely lost to the sporting public of Northampton because in the summer months he turned out as a middle order batsman/brilliant fielder for Northamptonshire County Cricket Club. Fanny made his debut in 1910. In comparison with his soccer career Walden's cricket achievements were modest, he never reached the 1.000 run milestone in a season and managed only five centuries in 435 innings. One of them came in a match against Surrey when Percy Fender thrashed the bowling for an amazing 35 minute century which rather overshadowed Fanny's efforts. In 1926 he did share in a record stand of 229 for the seventh wicket with Wilfred Timms, in a game versus Warwickshire. What he lacked batting he clearly made up for with his speed and brilliance fielding in the covers. Receiving a benefit in 1927, he retired two years later.

He joined the first class umpires list and worked his way up to the stand in eleven test matches. These included the 1938 match between England and Australia, when Len Hutton made the best test score of 364 at the Oval.

Fanny's umpiring came to an end with the outbreak of World War Two, like many of his contemporaries he became involved in the licensing trade and spent some time coaching schoolboys. He died in straightened circumstances on the 3rd May 1949. Unfortunately his business acumen was no match for his sporting skills.

His career statistics include:
1913-14 Footballer of the Year.

Two international caps for England.

Representative appearances for the Southern League and Football League XI's.

116 appearances and 27 goals for Northampton.

A first class batting average of 18.74.

114 wickets and 126 catches.

When looking for an 'epitaph' it would be brilliantly summed up in a 1914 headline from a Exeter paper, following a Cobblers' victory by four goals to nil.
"Wee Willie Walden works wonders."
Alliteration Heaven!
One of Walter's best friends Eric Tomkins survived the war, he represented the "air force" in games against the other services and guested for Spurs who wanted to sign him after the conflict. They baulked at Northampton's fee of £1200. He gained coaching qualifications and was at one point offered a job at Ajax which was turned down for domestic reasons. In 1938 he became a coach to Notts County but war intervened and he returned to Rushden as chief billeting officer. In 1946 he was offered a job with Hull City working with Fred Buckly but preferred to coach schoolboys for the Bedfordshire and Northamptonshire Education Authorities. Eric realistically noted the insecurity of professional football, "When you are successful you are safe, but as soon as things go wrong, you are out on your ear." In the course of a varied career he met many famous people, experienced highs and lows, worked in over a hundred schools. One honour he prized above all others was when Woodford Halse Secondary School named

one of their houses after him.
Hardly a character but a few words must be spared for the County Ground.The County Ground originally purchased in 1885 to be used for cricket, athletics and cycling - played host to Northamptonshire's debut in the minor counties championship in 1896. It had been hoped to develop it into one of the finest cricket grounds in England. However the “infant” Cobblers negotiated its use during the winter months and the infamous three sided soccer ground was conceived. This long lasting partnership effectively doomed the two participants to having the worst first class cricket ground and the worst league football venue in England. It is only since the Cobblers long awaited move to the Sixfields stadium that the original concept for cricket has begun to develop.
The old County Ground was a fond haunt of my younger days, the first fixture I recall attending was a fourth division game against Notts County, for much of the match I cheered the visitors little realising the Cobblers played in claret and white. In later years I remember consecutive victories 8-0 and 7-1 against Wrexham and Halifax respectively. A local cup tie versus Kettering Town attended by an astounding 22,000, I was hooked! Then the memorable rise to the old first division, the County Ground did indeed seem a theatre of dreams.
One can only imagine the horror of those first division stars during the 1965-66 season, the Cobblers one magical year in the top division, as they stared beyond the far touchline to the antiquated cricket pavilion and looked to the Spion Kop to see it so mercilessly abbreviated to accommodate the bowling club. George Best, Denis Law, Bobby Moore, Geoff Hurst, Alan Ball et al idly standing by as the poor ball boys chased hundreds of yards across the cricket square to retrieve hoofed clearances. Strangely the Country Ground was not the only three sided ground in the 1960's, Bramhall Lane, Sheffield shared that dubious distinction. Alan Birchenall in his auto biography “Bring Back the Birch” relates a simple situation when United were hanging onto a narrow lead the ball would

be wellied across to the cricket pavilion inevitably he who lives by the sword!

Scruffy and unkempt it was but the County Ground was packed with memories, from the first big soccer "gate", some 15,000 to see Sheffield United in January 1902 in the F.A. Cup to the final tearful farewells in 1994 (yes farewells) games against Chester, but with Sixfields not quite complete, again v. Mansfield. Other famous games would have to include the 1958 cup win over Arsenal, the horrendous 2-4 defeat by Fulham which hammered the final nail into the short stay in the top division. What about another F.A. Cup game 2-8 versus Manchester United when George Best returning from suspension scored six!

Once the Cobblers vacated the ground the cricket club was free to develop the football side and did so with great gusto, building a large indoor cricket school cum stand, straddling the old soccer pitch's centre circle. The ground has been developed so much recently that U.19 Tests and World Cup one day games have been staged. The original dream of the founding fathers, of a first rank cricket ground, is coming ever closer to fruition.

Walter's memorials are of course at the Cobblers' new home but his "spirit" and those of his contemporaries will always haunt the County Ground.

Herbert Chapman Walter's first manager at Northampton was to become one of the greatest managers ever. Having left Northampton, Chapman joined Leeds where he faced a similar situation as at Northampton with the team rock bottom of the second division. His first job was to secure enough votes for the club to avoid demotion. This was successfully accomplished and within two years he took the team to their highest position fourth.

Meanwhile international events took precedence Chapman continued as a manager and coupled this with work at an armaments factory. Football continued after a fashion during the war but was obviously restricted. Players, as they did between 1939 and 1945, guested for clubs that they were stationed near to. Payments were reduced to basic expenses and gate money was reduced by a percentage going to the war effort. It was a financial issue which led to Chapman leaving the club. In fact he left just before Leeds were expelled from the league for making illegal payments to players.

Chapman moved to Huddersfield first as secretary then eight months later he became manager. His first season in charge saw them win the FA Cup by beating Preston North End 1-0, at Stamford Bridge. Chapman continued to make shrewd signings, men like Clem Stephenson from Aston Villa who helped lead Huddersfield to an unprecedented three championships, although by the time the third was achieved Chapman had moved to Arsenal.

At Arsenal Chapman once again purchased an experienced player to build his team around. On this occasion it was Charlie Buchan from Sunderland. Once more his side went from strength to strength with cup final appearances in 1927, 1930 and 1933, championships in 1931 and 1933.

Sadly Chapman's devotion to football cost him his life. Whilst watching a game at Guildford he caught a chill from which he never recovered, he died on January 6th, 1934, a few months before Arsenal won the league again.

For me, Chapman's greatest achievement was signing Walter Tull!

Career Details

Isthmian League- Clapton F.C

1908-09	played	Goals
	15	10

Football League - Tottenham Hotspur

	Played	Goals
1909-10	7	1
1910-11	3	1
Total	10	2

Southern League - Northampton Town

	Played	Goals
1911-12	12	9
1912-13	28	-
1913-14	34	-
1914-15	31	-
Total	110	9

F.A. Cup - Northampton Town

	Played	Goals
1913-14	1	-
1914-15	2	-
Total	3	-
Professional Career Total	118	11

League Debut - Spurs v Sunderland (A)

1/9/09 Result 1-3

Final game v Arsenal (A)

8/4/11 Result 0-2

S. League Debut - Northampton v Watford (H)

21/10/11 Result 2-2

Final Game v Millwall (H)

1/5/15 Result 5-0

Club Records with Tull on books

	P	W	D	L	F	A	Pts	Pos	Team
1908-09	18	8	4	6	34	32	20	5th	Clapton
1909-10	38	11	10	17	53	69	32	15th	Spurs
1910-11	38	13	6	19	52	63	32	15th	"
1911-12	38	22	7	9	82	41	51	3rd	Northampton
1912-13	38	12	12	14	61	48	36	10th	"
1913-14	38	14	19	5	50	37	47	3rd	"
1914-15	38	16	11	11	56	51	43	5th	"

Walter Tull's Life and Times

1888 Walter Tull born Folkestone 28th April.
Preston North End win inaugural Football League Championship.

1889 Preston achieve league and cup "double".
London Docker's strike.

1897 Daniel died.

1898 Walter and Edward taken into care (Bonner Road).

1900 Edward adopted by the Warnock family.
Boxer rebellion in China.

1901 Queen Victoria dies.

1902 End of Boer War.

1903 Suffragette Movement founded.

1904 Walter leaves Bonner Road.

1908 Walter joins Clapton F.C.
GB beat Denmark to win Olympic Gold in soccer competition.

1909 Walter represents Clapton in AFA Cup Final.
Debut for Spurs on Argentinian Tour.
Bristol City debacle.
First Model T car.

1910 West Auckland F.C. retain Lipton Trophy.

1911 Walter signs for Northampton Town F.C.
Italy conquers Libya.
Manchester United win league championship.

1912 GB retain Olympic title, beating Denmark 4-2.
Sinking of the Titanic.

1914 Walter linked with Glasgow Rangers.
GB declares war on Germany.
Walter volunteers for army.

1915 Posted to France
Lusitania torpedoed.
Sheffield United win last "pre-war" F.A. Cup.
Everton league champions.

1916 Walter home on sick leave.
Officer training.
Easter Rebellion, Ireland.
First Battle of the Somme.

1917 Messines Ridge.
Passchendaele.
Walter posted to Italy.
Bolshevik Revolution in Russia.
USA entered the war.

1918 Walter killed in battle.
War ends 11/11/18.

Further Reading

Jack Alexander	McCrae's Battalion (Mainstream) 2003
Phill Ball:	Marbo (WSC)
Pat Barker:	The Ghost Road (Viking)
Brian Barron:	Fanny, Phil and Others (Byline)
Mark Beesley and Andy Roberts:	Cobblers On A Wing and a Prayer (Blayney)
Graham Betts:	Spurs, Day-to-Day Life At White Hart Lane (Mainstream)
Alan Birchenall	Bring Back the Birch (Polar)
Dave Bowler and Jas Bains:	Samba In The Smethwick End (Mainstream)
Malcolm Brown:	The Imperial War Museum Book Of The Somme (Pan)
Bryon Butler:	The Football League 1888-1988 (Macdonald Queen Anne Press)
Gordon Corrigan:	Sepoys in the Trenches (Spellmount)
Sebastian Faulks:	Birdsong (Vintage)
Eric Fowell:	A Picture View of Old Rushden (Fowell)

Frank Füredi: The Silent War (Pluto Press)

Frank Grande: Northampton Town F.C. The Official Centenary History 1897-1997 (Yore)

Colm Kerrigan: Gatling Gun George Hilsdon - London's First Football Star (A Rowe)

Ernest Hemmingway: A Farewell To Arms (Everyman)

Lyn MacDonald The Last Man, Spring 1918 (Penguin)

Martin Middlebrook: The Kaiser's Battle (Penguin)

Okokon Susan "Black Londoners 1880-1990" (Sutton)

Peter Oldham Messines Ridge (Lee Cooper)

N. Steel and P. Hart: Passchendaele - The Sacrificial Ground (Cassell)

Radd Andrew "100 Greats: Northamptonshire County Cricket Club" (Tempus)

Stephen Studd: Herbert Chapman Football Emperor (Souvenir)

Phil Vasili: Colouring Over The White Line (Mainstream)

Phil Vasili:	The First Black Footballer, Arthur Wharton 1865-1930. An Absence of Memory (Cass)
Walvin James	"The People's Game - the History Of Football Re-Visited" (Mainstream)
Ward A:	"Football's Strangest Matches" (Robson)